TRUTH OR CONSEQUENCES:

The Church in a Rearview Mirror

Second Edition

I0197230

The Battle for Beulah Land

Gene Triesch

Published by
Menorah Music Ministry Publishing
P O Box 958
Blanco, TX 78606

Author may be contacted at Menorah Music Ministry,
P O Box 958, Blanco, TX 78606
http://www.menorahmusic.com

To the One God of Abraham, Isaac and Jacob,

Yeshua, the Messiah,

be all praise, honor and glory!

To Him I give thanks for His written word and inspiration.

"Seek the LORD while He may be found,

Call upon Him while He is near.

Let the wicked forsake his way,

And the unrighteous man his thoughts;

Let him return to the LORD, And He will have mercy on him;

And to our God, For He will abundantly pardon.

For My thoughts are not your thoughts,

Nor are your ways My ways," says the LORD.

"For as the heavens are higher than the earth,

So are My ways higher than your ways,

And My thoughts than your thoughts.

For as the rain comes down, and the snow from heaven,

And do not return there, But water the earth,

And make it bring forth and bud,

That it may give seed to the sower and bread to the eater,

So shall My word be that goes forth from My mouth;

It shall not return to Me void, But it shall accomplish what I

please,

And it shall prosper in the thing for which I sent it."

Isaiah 55:6-11(NKJV)

To my wife, LaVada, I am deeply indebted.

This book would not have been possible without her inspiration and her computer and grammar skills. Thanks for your patience and the many hours of hard work entering the text and for being my locator for scriptures that I knew were there but couldn't come up with the 'where.'

May the God of Abraham, Isaac and Jacob use this collaborative effort for His honor and glory!

Many thanks to my daughter, Brandi, for "Sparky, the Smart Mouse" and for her comments and insight that helped to make this book more acceptable and readable to a wider audience.

---

[1] Handmade wooden cross/menorah, designed and created by Gene Triesch, Copyright 2004-Menorah Music Ministry

For his remarkable talent in photography, I am very grateful to my nephew, Willie Triesch, of WKT Photography, in Minneapolis, MN, for the unique cover art photo of the "church in a rearview mirror!" Thanks, Willie!

My gratitude for the hard work and editorial contributions by Wayne Gosnell and Harry Conger in both editions of *TRUTH OR CONSEQUENCES.* Wayne, thanks for your punctuation and editorial comments that helped to make this book just a little better, just a bit clearer, and just a bit easier to read! Harry, thanks for finding those little errors that just somehow seem to avoid detection. I am forever grateful to you both for your editorial skills and for your friendship!

THE OLD CORN HOUSE AT THE TRIESCH HOME PLACE[2]

FOREWORD

"Come and learn. You can't change the truth, but the truth can change you." This quote is fundamental to the understanding of the Old and New Testament scriptures. I wish I could take credit for it, but I can't. LaVada found it on the blog of a Jewish Rabbi.[3]

What is my purpose in writing an update to the first edition of *TRUTH OR CONSEQUENCES*? The primary purpose is to help build the faith of believers, assuring them that God is alive and at work in accomplishing His purpose and that they can rest assured that they can take Him at His Word. If you're reading this book out of curiosity or searching for answers in life, I hope that you will examine the evidence of Scripture presented and that His Spirit

---

[2] Image copyrighted 2004-Menorah Music Ministry, *The Old Corn House*
[3] Rabbi Nir Ben Artzi http://www.absolutetruth613.blogspot.co.il

would lead you in a quest for knowledge and truth. Perhaps you will begin to see the imprint of God's hand on history and His implementation of a plan that's been around for millennia.

I also want to call attention to and re-emphasize the importance of biblical prophecy and its implication for believers and nonbelievers alike with regard to historical and current world events. It could be that the Scriptures and comments contained herein will shed some light on a subject, which is too often confusing but more often ignored.

God doesn't change! Truth doesn't change! What has changed since the first edition of *TRUTH OR CONSEQUENCES* are conditions in the United States and conditions around the globe, particularly in regard to the Middle East. The world has become increasingly unstable. This edition includes updates of world events. It is difficult to keep events current because they change so quickly, but I have attempted to include those most relevant to God's plan for Israel.

I do not profess to have any special insight into the topics discussed in this book but have laid them out and arranged them in such a way as to attempt to make the subject matter less confusing. Here, I might be accused of taking Scripture out of context. If that is your opinion, let me encourage you to get out your Bible and prove whether or not that is what I have done.

This book contains information that I have gathered from many sources, which I consider to be reputable or I would not have used them. If it should turn out that I have included information that was not correct, I would appreciate being notified and, upon verification, will remove it from the digital copy and from future printed copies. Of course, there is my primary informational source, which is infallible in the original text and that is the Word of God!

The insights shared here are the result of many years of bible study and prayerful consideration in my search for Truth. I cannot explain why I have the desire to share this information other than that I believe it to be of great importance and I am led to do so. Some of the thoughts I present with regard to church traditions and doctrines may well be contrary to what is taught in traditional

Christianity. Please be assured it is not my intent to offend persons from any particular faith or denomination. God tells us through the prophet, Isaiah, *"Come, let us reason together..."* (Isaiah 1:18) I believe that there are people of faith in most every denomination who love the Truth and love the Lord, but far too few take the time to study Scripture and compare it to the practice and traditions of their church denomination.

It is essential in any business to take inventory. Likewise, it would be beneficial for a believer to take a *spiritual* inventory from time to time. Are your spiritual moorings based on biblical truth? And will the anchor hold in times of trouble? You should ask yourself, "Is my faith based on biblical truth or traditions of men?"

The Bible is about one-third prophecy. All Bible prophecy is related, in one way or another, to Israel, the people and the land. Although there are prophecies given concerning cities, empires and persons which are not necessarily Jewish or located in Israel, they were recorded by Hebrew prophets as an example and witness not only to Israel but also to Gentile nations that the God of Israel is the one and only true God. God emphasizes the importance of prophecy in the Book of Isaiah, *"Remember the former things of old, I am God and there is no other; I am God and there is none like me, declaring the end from the beginning and from ancient times things not yet done, saying my counsel shall stand and I will accomplish all my purpose (Isaiah 46:9-10)."* And Jesus emphasizes it also in the New Testament, *"Oh, foolish men, and slow of heart to believe all that the prophets have spoken (Luke 24:25)!"* When it comes to the word of God, we should prove all things in order to establish in our minds what is true. It is the Truth that sets us free. (John 8:32) It stands to reason then, that lies keep us in bondage!

The principal focus of this book is to emphasize the scriptural basis for Israel's right to the land of Israel and to expose the error in the anti-Semitic teachings of the Church. For centuries, many in Christianity as a whole have taken the teachings of early church leaders and passed them on to the next generation without regard as to whether they were true to Scripture. One particular teaching that I am referring to is that of "supercessionism," also called "replacement theology," or "the doctrine of spiritual Israel." This teaching, stated simply, is that God has replaced Israel with the

Church and that all the covenant promises He made to Israel now belong to the Church. As such, He has no present or future plans for Israel or the Jewish people. This theology led to the inclination for the "church" to separate itself from anything considered "Jewish" and, in so doing, separated itself from the very foundation of biblical truth—that foundation being the "Old" Testament (the Torah, the Prophets and the Writings)! I urge you to pay close attention to the Scriptures quoted herein which do not support this theology. In fact, there are hundreds of them and were I to include them all, this little book would not be quite so little and would require more than just a few hours of your time to read. What spiritual truths and blessings have been lost because of the Gentile church's efforts to distance itself from anything considered "Jewish?" I believe that by the time you've finished this "little book" you will have to agree that God has a plan He has had from the beginning and that He's sticking to it.

You may ask, "Why is this so important?" The short answer is that God says it is. The long answer would stretch down through about two thousand years of history in which no one knows how much death and destruction this lie has brought upon all of humanity. Anti-Semitism has its roots in replacement theology. One would have to concede that anti-Semitism played a major role in World War II. How many Jewish (and Gentile) lives were lost in that war alone? In Genesis 12:3, speaking to Abraham, God says, "*I will bless those who bless you and him who curses you, I will curse.*" We could certainly make the observation that the cursing of the Jews, the sons of Abraham through Isaac and Jacob, contributed to great destruction in Europe in the 20th century.

In the book of Numbers, Chapters 22 through 24, there is an interesting story about a prophet named Balaam. Balak, the king of Moab, sent messengers with financial incentives to hire Balaam to curse Israel as Balak thought this would make it possible for him to drive Israel from the land. Balaam inquired of God as to what to do with this request from Balak. God let him know he was not to go and curse this people. The request from the king of Moab came a second time and God allowed Balaam to go but it seemed that there was a question as to his motive and God was about to get his attention. On his way to meet Balak, the angel of the Lord got into the path of Balaam's donkey. The donkey could see the angel but Balaam could not. The donkey made every effort to avoid going near the angel on three occasions and, each time, was beaten by Balaam. Finally, God opened the donkey's mouth and she spoke to Balaam saying something like, "Why are you beating me? Haven't I always been obedient and followed your commands for all these many years?" When Balaam answered "yes" he, too, was able to see the angel who had been put there to kill him. His life was spared on three occasions because his donkey had eyes to see!

Understandably, the incident caught Balaam's attention. From that time on, he would be sure not to say or do anything without God's instruction. When he met Balak, Balaam was probably still shaking when he told him he would only be able to speak the words that God had given him—and nothing else!

On three different occasions, Balaam was asked by Balak to curse Israel and each time he responded with God's word. One response was, *"How can I curse whom God has not cursed?...*(Numbers 23:8)" Then in Numbers 23:19 (NIV), he said, **"God is not a man that He should lie, nor a son of man, that he should change His mind. Does He speak and then not act? _Does He promise and not fulfill?_ "**

I remember when I was about ten or twelve years old how absolutely hilarious I thought it was to see "Frances, The Talking Mule" in a movie theater. If we were able to stand by and see Balaam and his donkey talking back to him, we would likely have that same reaction. We might ask ourselves, "Is it necessary for God to put a donkey with the gift of speech and eyes that are not veiled in our path before we can see and believe what He says in His word?"

In the 31st chapter of Numbers, God instructed Moses and Israel to take vengeance on the Midianites. Balaam apparently hung out with the Midianites a little too long, and as a consequence, met an untimely death along with five Midianite kings. He was keeping high company! His love for financial gain from sources that were opposed to God's plan for Israel had fatal consequences. Such was the fate of this "prophet for hire."[4]

---

[4] 2 Peter 2:15-16

In the Book of Esther, a similar story is unveiled where an evil man named Haman devises a plan to exterminate all the Jews in Persia. Queen Esther's uncle, Mordecai, exposes the plot and Esther was able to persuade the king to issue a decree to save the Jews. As a consequence, Haman was hanged on the gallows he had constructed to hang Mordecai! Ancient Persia is the country we know today as Iran. Iran is seeking nuclear capabilities and its leaders have on numerous occasions called for the destruction of Israel. Will the haters of the God of Israel ever learn?

Do we, as believers, bless the descendants of Abraham, Isaac, and Jacob or dare we continue to skirt around and ignore what He prophesied so long ago?

TABLE OF CONTENTS

1 - BEULAH, THE BUZZER!   13

2 – A BRIEF REVIEW OF HEBREW HISTORY   22

3 - GOD'S PLAN – PROPHETS OF THE OLD TESTAMENT   28

4 - THE NEW TESTAMENT   49

5 - THE NEW TESTAMENT AND PAUL'S TEACHING   57

6 - WHICH LAW, PAUL?   65

7 - PERSECUTION OF CHRISTIANS AND JEWS   78

8 - IN GOD'S TIME   84

9 - MODERN ISRAEL: THE "BULLY" OF THE MIDDLE EAST??   94

10 - CHURCH DOCTRINE INSTITUTIONALIZES HATRED   117

11 - REFORMATION, HOLOCAUST AND REPENTANCE   129

12 - AGAINST THE PURPOSE OF GOD   147

13 - WHERE IS THE WISE MAN?   153

14 - PETER, PAUL AND PROPHECY   165

15 - ON THE ROAD TO EMMAUS   179

Addendum   198

CHAPTER ONE

BEULAH, THE BUZZER!

Beulah, the Buzzer! Americans under the age of thirty-five are not likely to remember the game show, "Truth or Consequences." This show began on radio in 1940 and on television in 1950 and was quite popular until its final production in 1978. In general, the host of the show would ask the contestants a trivia question to which they were not likely to know the answer. After a specified time, "Beulah, the Buzzer," would sound. The contestants would then be faced with the "consequences" if they responded incorrectly or failed to respond in the allotted time. Being a "fun" show, the consequence would normally be a favorable or welcome surprise. Wouldn't it be great if that were the only consequence of not knowing the truth??

What is truth? Is it important? And just how important is it? Does it matter whether or not we spend our lives acknowledging some of what is true and not all of what is true? What are the consequences of embracing partial truth? Where do we find what is true? Jesus said, *"...I am the Way, the Truth and the Life; no one comes to the Father, but by me* (John 14:6)." The Bible says that Satan is the father of lies[5] and he has been propagating them for millennia. I propose to you that the question, "What is Truth?" is the most important question in the history of the world. Life on this earth and life eternal depend on one's understanding of the answer!

The God of the Bible doesn't ask for much...only that we put Him first! In other words, we should NOT place anyone or anything ahead of God in our priorities. For He said, *"You shall have no other gods before Me (Exodus 20:3)."* For that

---

[5] John 8:44

we receive His blessings and favor! What are God's blessings? His blessings include all that we have need of... food, shelter, clothing, protection, freedom, love, joy, peace, and when necessary, even discipline. Discipline reminds us to return to His protection. The greatest of His blessings is love![6]

God's word was recorded over many centuries by numerous authors referred to as prophets in the Old Testament and as disciples or apostles in the New Testament. God reveals His character in the Bible. Christianity is based on the Old and New Testaments while Judaism is based solely on the Old Testament (Hebrew scriptures). The Bible is, in all probability, not only the most ancient recorded history of mankind, but also, a history of God's love for mankind and God's desire to reestablish a relationship with man which was broken with the fall of Adam.

His plan was and is to do this through a people chosen for that purpose. They were chosen because they were descendants of a man God named Abraham. God established a covenant with Abraham because he was found to believe and have faith in the God whom he could not see or touch! It's relatively easy to believe in what we can see or touch but what about what we can't see or touch? Abraham had that kind of faith! Abraham's faith was active in that he kept God's statutes and commandments and was obedient when asked to offer his son as a sacrifice upon the altar.[7] While on the way to the sacrifice, Isaac asked his father, *"Where is the lamb for a burnt offering?"* He responded that, *"God will provide himself the lamb...*(Genesis 22:7-8)."* At that time God provided a ram. The "lamb" was still to come! God's covenant with Abraham included blessings of land, nations,[8] and descendants who were to number as many as the stars.[9] God told him to leave the

---

[6] 1 Corinthians 13:4-7
[7] James 2:21
[8] Genesis 17:5,8
[9] Genesis 22:17

14

country in which he lived and go to a land that he would be shown. He responded in faith.

An interesting scenario is outlined in *The Israel People – A Study, Book I*.[10] The author references the ancient Hebrew writings of the Book of Jubilees, believed to be written in the first century, A.D., and the Book of Jasher which is referenced in the Old Testament in Joshua 10:13 and II Samuel 1:18. According to both of these books, after the flood there was a dividing of territories to each of the sons of Noah — Shem, Ham and Japheth. Ham's son, Canaan, saw the land that had been allotted to Shem, liked that land and decided to settle there. His brothers and his father said that he would be cursed in the land because that land belonged to Shem. Abraham was a direct descendant of Shem. Thus, this land, to which God had instructed Abraham to go, was truly a "promised land." When Joshua led Israel into the Promised Land, that land was the land originally given to Shem and later promised to Abraham. Perhaps this gives us an insight as to why Abraham was to go to the land of Canaan. Not only were the inhabitants to be displaced because of their pagan gods and culture, it is possible that the land where they lived wasn't theirs to begin with!

God's covenant with Abraham was passed on to his son and grandson, Isaac and Jacob. Jacob's name was changed to Israel, which became the name of this chosen people and their story is recorded in the Old Testament. Interwoven within this story are hundreds of prophecies pointing to Jesus, who was prophesied to be of the tribe of Judah[11] (thus, he was "Jewish"), descended from Israel's King David,[12] and who

---

[10] The Israel People – A Study, Book I, by D. M. Jamison, Shepherd Publishing House, P O Box 1481, Nogales, AZ 85628
[11] Genesis 49:10
[12] Isaiah 9:7

would be Savior and Redeemer for all mankind[13]—the lamb slain from the foundation of the world.[14]

My Prophecy Study Bible[15] lists over a hundred prophecies with regard to the first coming of Jesus and over three hundred with regard to His second coming. The first coming prophecies were made hundreds of years before the birth of Christ and were often very specific. Here are a few of them:

Scripture	Prophecy	Sriptural Fulfillment
Isaiah 7:14	To be born of a virgin	Matthew 1:18 & 1:23-25;
	To be named Immanuel	Luke 1:26-35; 7:16
Micah 5:2	To be born in Bethlehem	Matthew 2:1
Psalm 72:10	Wise men to bring gifts	Matthew 2:11
Zechariah 9:9	To enter Jerusalem riding donkey	Matthew 21:6-11; Luke 19:35-37
Zechariah 11:12	To be betrayed for 30 pieces of silver	Matthew 26:14-15
Zechariah 12:10	His hands, feet and side to be pierced	John 19:34; 20:27
Psalms 22:16	Same as above	
Psalms 22:18	Soldiers to cast lots for His clothes	Matthew 27:35; Mark 15:24; Luke 23:24; John 19:24

The odds for this many prophecies, made hundreds of years prior to this person's birth, to come true in the person, Jesus of Nazareth, would have to be considered mathematically impossible and beyond comprehension.

Over hundreds of years, God's relationship with His people, Israel, was one of wrath for disobedience and unbelief, but more so, of grace and mercy every time they would acknowledge Him and seek to walk in the "way" that He had prescribed for them, i.e., follow His instructions. Because of the very nature of God and the design of man in "God's" image, this "way" was the path necessary to walk so as to

---

[13] Isaiah 52:10

[14] Revelation 13:8

[15] The Prophecy Study Bible, KJV, AMG Publishers, (Dates of 2166-516 B.C.)

receive His blessings and favor. And yet, God has designed man with free will. He doesn't want man's adoration and love as a consequence of a robotic reaction. Man must choose between good and evil -- obedience, or disobedience. There are those who may unknowingly follow some of God's instructions because of an innate desire to do good, demonstrating their love for others. As a consequence they receive His blessings, not realizing from where those blessings came. God is not a respecter of persons.[16]

It is God's desire and will to establish a relationship of peace and love and He has demonstrated this in His plan to save humanity from sin (transgression of God's Law/Torah[17]) that was inherited from Adam. *"For God so loved the world that He gave His only begotten Son, that whoever believes in Him should not perish but have eternal life (John 3:16)."* This is all recorded and prophesied as scripture says, "from the beginning."

In Old Testament times God revealed Himself through His servants, the prophets. In fact, He says that He does nothing without revealing it to His servants the prophets.[18] Prophets who made prophecies that did not come to pass, or if they made prophecies that weren't popular, were often put to death. Prophecy was a serious business! In recent times, many Christians have been "burned," so to speak, by prophecy teachers who have "set dates" when making predictions that did not come true. As a result, many people have heard "the sky is falling" one too many times — could this be a Satanic setup? This gives real meaning to Peter's prophecy in 2 Peter 3:3-4, *"First of all you must understand this, that scoffers will come in the last days with scoffing, following their own passions and saying, 'where is the promise of His coming? For*

---

[16] 2 Peter 10:34
[17] 1 John 3:4
[18] Amos 3:7

ever since the fathers fell asleep, all things have continued as they were from the beginning of creation."

Bible prophecy fulfilled is God's "exclamation point!!!" Sort of, "I told you so long ago!" Nowhere in the Bible does it record that God ever said "Oops!!" He does say, *"I the Lord do not change. So you, O descendants of Jacob <u>are not destroyed</u>* (Malachi 3:6 NIV)." Listen to what Jesus says in Luke 24:25... *"Oh, foolish men, and <u>slow of heart to believe all that the prophets have spoken!</u>"* About 750 B.C. God revealed Himself through the prophet Isaiah, but with a "challenge." In Isaiah 41:21-24 and 44:6-7, God said that if there should be any gods like Himself, let <u>them</u> proclaim what is to come.

Isaiah 44:6-7
Thus says the Lord, the King of Israel and His Redeemer, the Lord of Hosts; "I am the first and the last; besides Me there is no God. <u>Who is like me? Let him proclaim it, let him declare and set it forth before me. Who has announced from of old the things to come?</u> ***Let them tell us what is yet to be.***"

In other words, put it down in writing, as I have done, so that future generations will have concrete evidence as to who is the one true God. Only the God of creation would be able to give us an accurate outline for the history of His Chosen People from the beginning of time to the end of the age. None have successfully accepted that challenge. Note God's words, *"I am the first and the last."* Those are exactly the words as recorded by John that Jesus spoke in the Book of Revelation.

Revelation 1:8
I am the Alpha and the Omega," says the Lord God, who is and who was and who is to come, the Almighty.

Revelation 1:17
...Fear not, I am the first and the last.

Revelation 22:12-13
Behold, I am coming soon, bringing my recompense, to repay everyone for what he has done. I am the Alpha and the Omega, the first and the last, the beginning and the end.

[Note: *Alpha* and *Omega* in Greek is the same as the Hebrew, *Alef* and *Tav,* i.e., the first and the last.]

Isaiah 46:9-10
Remember the former things of old, I am God and there is no other; I am God and there is none like me, declaring the end from the beginning and from ancient times things not yet done, saying my counsel shall stand and I will accomplish all my purpose.

God emphasizes His prophetic word, sovereignty, and purpose in Chapter 46. Then in Chapter 48, He says He will accomplish His purpose suddenly.

Isaiah 48:3
The former things I declared of old, they went forth from my mouth and I made them known; then suddenly I did them and they came to pass.

Satan is the master of lies and deception. He has been using and confusing man since the beginning when he told Eve, *"Hath God said?"*[19] In other words, *"Aw, c'mon! He didn't really mean that!"* He has been leading man to create so-called gods that conform to man's idea of who and what they think God should be. So often, just enough truth is thrown into the mix, so as to make it more difficult to determine "what is Truth?" This would have been all the more reason to issue the challenge as written in Isaiah, *"Tell us what is to come hereafter (Isaiah 41:23)!"*

---

[19] Genesis 3:1-5

In the next chapter we'll take a look at a summary of the history of a people whom God had chosen to reveal to the world His purpose for humanity. But first, a short detour...

✳ ✳ ✳ ✳

On a personal note...

At the end of several chapters in this book, I will deviate slightly from the text with related information, commentary, or a personal note. Is it coincidence that I am around to research scripture, gather information, put it together in a book and then share it with the readers? Probably not! On more than one occasion, my life could well have been cut short. As a child of about seven or eight, I fell about twenty feet from a barn, head first, onto a plow. The wound required over twenty stitches and I still have a scar! Had I been minding my chores, as my dad said, this would not have happened. However, my brother and cousins and myself were sure having a lot of fun in that hayloft!

As a young man in the mid-sixties, I was shot in the neck accidentally. I will tell you more about that in the next note. But, about ten years later, I was driving an old VW bug on a narrow two-lane highway with my three-year old daughter as a passenger. An oncoming car pulled into my lane to pass another vehicle. Fortunately, the oncoming car took the ditch to my right and I passed between the two oncoming vehicles! I checked my rearview mirror and saw that the driver of that oncoming car was able to regain control of his vehicle and get back onto the highway. The little bug that we were in was one that had no seatbelts and the gas tank was under the hood in front of the car! The odds of survival in a head-on collision would have been pretty slim.

In January 2003, I had surgery for the removal of colon cancer. Gifted hands removed the cancer and I am free of the disease. In November 2010, a year after the release of the first edition of this book, *TRUTH OR CONSEQUENCES,* I was making repairs on a roof and fell off and broke my neck. After surgery, two doctors said that I shouldn't have survived this injury. And yet, I did survive, and without paralysis. Recovery time was slow, but in a little over a year, I was almost as good as new! Indeed, has all this been a coincidence?

Sometimes things happen in life to give one cause to reflect. I guess you could say that I have had my share of them. In reflection, I can see God's Hand of Protection on my life. Why? I have wondered what I've done with my life that could be considered helpful to my family, friends and neighbors. This book is an effort to have a positive impact on those who may read it. I pray that it may give the reader a reason to reflect and to be inspired to search for **Truth**. Truth is found in the Word of God and it is the *Truth* that sets us free!

CHAPTER TWO
A BRIEF REVIEW OF HEBREW HISTORY

Don't panic, you're not going to have a quiz on years, dates and names at the end of this chapter! It may, however, be helpful if you can get a grasp of names and the sequence of events as revealed in the Bible. This may be helpful for your understanding. If you are already knowledgeable of this history, perhaps it will be a helpful review.

2166 B.C. – 1948 A.D.

THE PATRIARCHS
- Abraham, born 2166 B.C. [20]
- Isaac, born 2066 B.C.
- Jacob, born 2006 B.C. - Name changed to Israel.[21]

He had twelve sons [22] who became the twelve tribes of the nation Israel, Levi being a priestly tribe interspersed in their midst.[23] Joseph became two tribes,[24] namely, Ephraim and Manasseh. Jacob's favorite son, Joseph, was sold by his brothers into slavery in Egypt,[25] where he became the second highest ruler in Egypt[26] and saved his family from starvation.[27] For over 350 years these families grew and became a multitude. In 1730 B.C. they were enslaved in Egypt[28] and remained so until 1447 B.C.

---

[20] The Prophecy Study Bible, KJV, AMG Publishers, (Dates of 2166-516 B.C.)
[21] Gen. 32:28
[22] Gen. 35:22-26
[23] Num. 8:5-19, Deut. 33:10, I Chron. 6:54-81
[24] Gen. 48:5
[25] Gen. 37:28
[26] Gen. 41:37-45
[27] Gen. 42 & 43
[28] Ex. 1:8-14

- In 1447 B.C., Moses led Israel in the exodus[29] and, because of their unbelief spent 40 years in the wilderness.[30]
- In 1407 B.C. Joshua led Israel into Canaan, the Promised Land.[31]
- In 1375-1050 B.C., Israel was ruled by judges.[32] The people were not happy with judges and wanted to be ruled by a king like the nations around them. Subsequently, Saul became the first king of Israel and ruled for 40 years.[33]
- In 1010 B.C., David became king of Israel and ruled for 40 years.[34]
- In 970 B.C., Solomon, David's son, became king, ruled for 40 years and built the first Jewish temple.[35]
- In 931 B.C., after Solomon's death, the kingdom was divided.[36]
- The northern kingdom (ten tribes) was called Israel – the capitol was Samaria.[37]
- The southern kingdom (two tribes) was called Judah – the capitol was Jerusalem.[38]
- They were separate nations ruled by separate kings.
- Jeroboam, the first king of the northern kingdom of Israel, was fearful that the people would return to the temple in Jerusalem and he would lose his power over them. So, he changed the feast days of Israel, established his own temples of worship and they began worshiping false gods. He appointed priests from among the people who were not Levites. The Levitical priests then returned to Judah.[39] Ultimately, God declared that He divorced

---

[29] Ex. 12:15
[30] Ex. 3:10, Jos. 5:6
[31] Joshua 3
[32] Judges 2:16
[33] I Samuel 11:15
[34] II Samuel 5:3-4, I Kings 2 11
[35] I Kings 1:43-46, I Kings 11:42
[36] I Kings 12:16-20
[37] II Kings 3:1, II Kings 10:36, II Kings 15:8, II Kings 17:1
[38] I Kings 14:21, II Chronicles 10:5-12
[39] I Kings 12:25-33, II Chronicles 11:13-14

Israel the northern kingdom, which was also referred to as Ephraim. [40] In 722 B.C., Israel was conquered by Assyria and dispersed[41] (removed from their land). After their dispersion, they lost their identity and thus, became known as the "lost tribes of Israel."

- **On the 9th day of Av** (Hebrew Calendar), in 586 B.C., Solomon's temple was destroyed and Judah, the southern kingdom, was conquered by the Babylonian king, Nebuchadnezzar, and was exiled to Babylon.[42] When Cyrus, king of Persia, conquered Babylon in 538 B.C., some of the Jews were allowed to return to begin rebuilding the temple.[43] The prophet Isaiah prophesied that Cyrus would be God's "servant" some 200 years prior to this event.[44] The temple was completed by Zerubbabel[45] in 516 B.C., however, it could in no way be compared to the one that Solomon had built.[46] It was added to over the years, but deteriorated in time. In 20 B.C., King Herod began building a temple that did rival Solomon's temple. This temple was the temple where Jesus and his disciples taught. However, the outer courts of this temple were not completed until 64 A.D., just six years before it was destroyed by the Romans.

- Over the centuries, Judah was ruled by Babylon, the Medes and Persians, the Greeks, and by Rome before and after Jesus. Judah had a very brief period of self governance after the Maccabee revolt in 168 B.C. They rebelled after their temple had been defiled by Antiochus Epiphanes, King of the Seleucid Empire, which was one of the divisions of Alexander's Greek Empire. Judas Maccabee liberated Jerusalem and rededicated the temple

---

[40] Jeremiah 3:6-8
[41] II Kings 17:6 and 22-23
[42] II Kings 25
[43] II Chronicles 36:22-23
[44] Isaiah 44:28
[45] Ezra 5:2 and 6:15
[46] Ezra 3:12

in 165 B.C.,[47] with an eight day celebration to commemorate the Feast of Tabernacles (Sukkot), which they had not been able to celebrate at the appointed time due to the war of liberation. At the time of this rededication, according to rabbinical "tradition," the seven branch menorah burned for eight days on one day's supply of oil. The rededication of the temple began what is known today as the Festival of Hanukkah, which is Hebrew for the word "dedication." This festival provides the historical basis for the nine branch Hanukkah menorah. The Maccabean revolt is recorded in the book of Maccabees, an extra-biblical ancient Jewish text. Some bibles include it in the Apocrypha.

• Roman rule began in 63 B.C. Judea, the Greco-Roman name for the tribe of Judah, was often in a state of rebellion to Roman rule. The Jews were evicted and dispersed the second time in 70 A.D., at which time the Romans destroyed the second Jewish temple... destroyed once again **on the 9th of Av.** Roman Emperor Hadrian allowed Jews to return to Jerusalem in 118 A.D. with the possibility of rebuilding the temple, but quickly reneged on the idea, which soon led to another rebellion. For 65 years, the on and off rebellion of the Jews led to the completion of the dispersion when the Bar-Kokhba Revolt was crushed in 135 A.D. As an act of spite, Hadrian changed the name of Judea (Judah) to "Syria Palestina."[48] [49]

• 'Dispersion' sounds like a rather benign event. Actually, hundreds of thousands of Jews died in the wars connected to these dispersions.

---

[47] The Silent Centuries, The So-Called "Intertestamental" Period, A Study of the 400 Years Between Malachi and Matthew by Al Maxey, http://www.zianet.com/maxey/InterLst.htm, maxey@zianet.com.
[48] The name was changed to "Syria Palestina" (Palestine), *The Jewish Virtual Library,* https://www.jewishvirtuallibrary.org/jsource/Judaism/revolt1.html Accessed September 2, 2015
[49] A rendering of "Philistia," the ancient enemies of Israel, the Philistines.

- The land of Israel was primarily under Arab and Islamic rule from about the mid-seventh century until 1099 when European Christians gained control as a result of the Crusades. The Christians maintained control through the year 1291,[50] at which time Islamic forces of the Ottoman Empire regained control and ruled until British General Edmond Allenby liberated Jerusalem in 1917.[51]

Here, I'd like to ask a question! What are the odds of an event involving such an important aspect of the Jewish faith, namely the temple being destroyed, happening on exactly the same date 656 years apart? **The 9th of Av** is a special day of abstention, fasting and mourning for the Jewish people because, not only were both temples destroyed on that day, but seven additional catastrophic events in Jewish history have all happened on this same day of the year.[52] How could that be coincidence?

The 9th of Av in Jewish History[53]

- **Av 9, 1445 BC** – During Israel's exodus from Egypt, the ten spies sent into the promised land brought a fearful negative report of giants in the land leading to 40 years of wandering in the wilderness. Of the ten, only Caleb and Joshua trusted the LORD and had the attitude, "We can do this!" or, in other words, "We can take possession of the land!"
- **Av 9, 586 BC** - Babylonians destroy Solomon's temple.
- **Av 9, 70 AD** - Romans destroy 2nd temple.
- **Av 9, 135 AD** - The Bar-Kokhba revolt was crushed by Roman Emperor Hadrian. The city of Betar -- the Jews' last stand against the Romans -- was captured and liquidated. Over 100,000 Jews were slaughtered.

---

[50] History.com/topics/crusades - *Crusades*
[51] Prophecy in the News, 2008, article by J. R. Church, *After Centuries of Exile, They Come Home!* – Page 34
[52] B'rit Hadasha Messianic Jewish Synagogue, Memphis, TN, http://www.brithadasha.org/9thofAv.htm
[53] http://www.watchmanbiblestudy.com/BibleStudies/Definitions/Feasts/Def_Tisha_BAv.htm

- **Av 9, 1290 AD** - July 25, 1290 Jews forced out of England.
- **Av 9, 1492 AD** – July 31, 1492 Jews forced out of Spain.
- **Av 9, 1914 AD** - August 1, 1914 World War I began (Germany declared war on Russia.)
- **Av 9, 1942 AD** - July 23, 1942 - Treblinka extermination camp opened in occupied Poland, east of Warsaw.
- **Av 9, 2005 AD - Gaza Evacuation: The Beginning of Dividing Israel for Peace** Starting at midnight on August 14, 2005, the entry and presence of Israeli citizens in the areas to be evacuated was prohibited under paragraph 22A of the Implementation of the Disengagement Plan Law 2005. Disengagement from the Gaza Strip was completed on August 22, and from northern Samaria on August 23, 2005.

Going into the next chapter, let's recall the history of the patriarchs and pick up their story in Egypt where His Chosen People, the descendents of Jacob who after about 400 years had grown into a multitude, were now in bondage. God heard their cry, knew their suffering and was about to send deliverance.[54]

---

[54] Exodus 3:7-8

CHAPTER THREE

GOD'S PLAN – PROPHETS OF THE OLD TESTAMENT

Most everyone has heard the Old Testament story of Moses[55] and how his Hebrew mother placed him in a basket among the reeds on the Nile River in order to save his life. He was found by the daughter of Pharaoh who took him as her own to raise. She sought out a mother, who just happened to be the child's birth mother, to nurse this child. As we see later in this story, God had a plan and was orchestrating these events. Moses was raised as an Egyptian in the house of Pharaoh but later got into trouble for killing an Egyptian who was beating one of his kinsmen, a Hebrew slave. Moses fled to another country, got married, had children and became a shepherd. While attending his sheep, he had an encounter with an angel of the Lord as the word of God spoke to him from a burning bush. When told to go back to Egypt and lead the Hebrews out of slavery into the land of Canaan, his first response was something like, "Who, me? Who am I to go to the great Pharaoh of Egypt?" Moses was, however, obedient and did as God commanded. Many, especially the Jews, consider him to be the greatest prophet of Israel. He is credited with recording the first five books of the Bible.

This story of Moses continues God's covenant with Abraham, Isaac and Jacob—his covenant with the children of Israel. The vast majority of people worldwide are unaware that this story continues to be revealed. Just as in the days of Moses, God's plan continues to unfold. Let's move forward and examine that plan. Perhaps we can begin to get a grasp on God's prophetic word.

---

[55] Exodus Chapters 2-4

Through His prophets, God's word foretold of Israel's and Judah's destruction and dispersion because of their disobedience and idolatry. There were to be great blessings for obedience and horrific curses for disobedience. In Deuteronomy 29, God issued instructions for Israel to come into covenant as His people, but warned of the consequences for failure to live up to this covenant. Before they entered Canaan in 1407 B.C., as recorded in Deuteronomy, Moses spoke to all Israel.

Deuteronomy 29:10-28

10 You stand this day all of you before the Lord your God...

12 that you may enter into the sworn covenant of the Lord your God...

13 that He may establish you this day as His people...

14 Nor is it with you only that I make this sworn covenant,

15 but with him who is not here with us this day as well as with him who stands here with us this day before the Lord our God.

18 Beware lest there be among you a man or woman or family or tribe, whose heart turns away this day from the Lord our God to go and serve the gods of those nations;... [pagan gods.]

22 And the generation to come, your children who rise up after you, and the foreigner who comes from a foreign land, would say, when they see the affliction of that land...that the Lord has made it sick—

23 the whole land brimstone and salt, a burnt out waste, unsown, and growing nothing, where no grass can sprout...

This curse on the land of Israel was the actual condition of that land for about 2000 years and it remained that way until the Jewish people returned in the 20th century.

24 yea, all the nations would say, 'Why has the Lord done thus to this land?'...

25 Then man would say, 'It is because they forsook the covenant of the Lord, the God of their fathers...

27 therefore the anger of the Lord was kindled against this land, bringing upon it all the curses written in this book;

28 and the Lord uprooted them from their land...and cast them into another land...

In Verse 15, Moses says that Israel is entering into a covenant with God to be established as His people. Not with Israel only, but also with him who was not there that day. Who do you suppose He was referring to? Gentiles, perhaps? Or, maybe you and me? God warns Israel that they were not to serve other gods and in Verse 22 speaks of a generation to come as well as foreigners who were to be a witness. Note that from Verse 22 through 28, Moses is speaking of the future in the past tense. God prerecorded Israel's failure to keep this covenant. Moses continues...

Deuteronomy 30:1-5

1 And when all these things come upon you, the blessing and the curse, which I have set before you, and you call them to mind among all the nations where the Lord your God has driven you,

2 and return to the Lord your God,...

3 then the Lord your God will restore your fortunes, and have compassion upon you, and He will gather you again from all the peoples where the Lord your God has scattered you.

4 If your outcasts are in the uttermost parts of heaven, from there the Lord your God will gather you...

5 and the Lord your God will bring you into the land which your fathers possessed...

But He also prerecorded their restoration. Note that no matter where His people had been driven, God was going to gather them again. This indicates that they had been gathered before as was the case when they were brought back from Babylon about 516 B.C. History reveals that Judah was scattered among the nations again by the Roman Empire in 70 and 135 A.D.

Amos 9:8-9

... "I will not utterly destroy the house of Jacob," says the Lord. For lo, I will command, and shake the house of Israel among all the nations as one shakes with a sieve, but no pebble shall fall upon the earth.

Hosea 5:15 and 6:1-2

I will return again to my place, until they acknowledge their guilt and seek my face, and in their distress they seek me, saying, "Come let us return to the Lord; for He has torn, that He may heal us; He has stricken, and He will bind us up. After two days He will revive us; on the third day, He will raise us up, that we may live before Him."

After the resurrection, Jesus/Yeshua, the I AM[56] and the Word who was with God from the beginning,[57] ascended and thus returned to heaven to sit at the right hand of the Father. *"I will return again to my place..."* God's Word says that, with the Lord, a day is as a thousand years and a thousand years is as a day as referenced in 2 Peter 3:8 and Psalm 90:4. Remember also that it's been about 2000 years since the death, burial and resurrection of Yeshua— just the day before yesterday — or, two days in God's time. The third day will be His millennial reign!

Jesus' mother would have called him by the Hebrew name she was instructed to give Him at birth, *Yeshua*, which means salvation. Hereafter in this book, I may refer to Him, as either Jesus or Yeshua.

---

[56] John 8:58
[57] John 1:1

Micah 5:2-3 (NKJV)

But you, Bethlehem Ephrathah, Though you are little among the thousands of Judah, Yet out of you shall come forth to Me The One to be Ruler [Jesus/Yeshua] *in Israel, Whose goings forth are from of old, From everlasting. Therefore He* [Jesus/Yeshua] *shall give them up, Until the time that she who is in labor has given birth; then the remnant of His brethren shall return to the children of Israel.*

Yeshua to give up Judah until she who is in labor has given birth? Israel reborn as a nation? May 14, 1948?? Just think about it! The Jewish people have certainly had enough suffering and affliction in the diaspora to be considered in labor, the holocaust being the climax. It is not such a stretch to come to the conclusion that the holocaust was the last great labor pain before the birth of the nation, Israel.

Isaiah 66:7-8

Before she was in labor she gave birth; before her pain came upon her she was delivered of a son. Who has heard such a thing? Who has seen such things? Shall a land be born in one day? Shall a nation be brought forth in one moment? <u>*For as soon as Zion was in labor,*</u> *she brought forth her sons.*

Here the prophet Isaiah refers to the birth of Jesus and he also uses the illustration of birth pains to describe the rebirth of the nation of Israel, a nation that was brought forth suddenly. When? As soon as Zion was in labor! Who has ever heard or seen anything like this, he asks. His inference is that this is truly a miracle. Never in the history of nations has a nation been completely destroyed and dispersed around the world and yet, somehow, manage to maintain an identity for almost 2000 years, and then be reborn as a nation. Prophecy fulfilled!

Isaiah 11:10-12

*In that day the root of Jesse shall stand as an ensign to the peoples; Him shall the nations seek, and His dwellings shall be glorious. In that day the Lord will extend His hand <u>yet a second time</u> to recover the remnant which is left of His people, from Assyria, from Egypt, from Pathros, from Ethiopia, from Elam, from Shinar, from Hamath, and from the coastlands of the sea. He will **raise an ensign** [flag] for the nations, and will assemble the outcasts of Israel, and gather the dispersed of Judah <u>from the four corners of the earth</u>.*

Let's look at that word, "ensign"…God will raise up "an ensign", a flag, for the nations. We could certainly say that we are living "in that day" when God has raised the flag of Israel for the nations. The design of that flag came about in the late 1800s and early 1900s. Four people, individually, had the same vision (idea) for that flag. Two were in the United States, one in Switzerland and one in Israel. The design was adopted by the Israeli Council of State October 28, 1948[58]. The flag of Israel is basically a white prayer shawl with two horizontal blue stripes along the border separated by a blue Star of David in its center. The "root of Jesse" is obviously a reference to Jesse's son, King David, and thus, God has basically given the design of the Israeli flag in the previous scripture. What could be a more descriptive banner for Israel than a piece of cloth used as a prayer covering for the Jewish people which displays the Star of David, the sign of the "root of Jesse?"

Now, let's consider God extending His hand "yet a second time"…Many in the Church today believe that "<u>all prophecy</u>" concerning God regathering the Jews took place after their dispersion to Babylon in 586 B.C. But this scripture is not speaking of God regathering the Jews from Babylon in the first

---

[58] <u>Lamplighter</u>, May/June 2008, *The Story Behind Israel's Flag*, by Dr. David Reagan

dispersion. How could the "four corners of the earth" be considered as a specific place called Babylon? As clearly stated, God extended His hand to recover the remnant of His people, the outcasts of Israel and the dispersed of Judah a second time from the four corners of the earth.

Isaiah 62:10-11

*Go through, go through the gates, prepare the way for the people; build up, build up the highway, clear it of stones, **lift up an ensign** over the peoples. Behold, the Lord has proclaimed to the end of the earth; say to the daughter of Zion, "Behold your Salvation [Yeshua] comes; behold, his reward is with him and his recompense before him."*

Let's lift up that flag again and notice that Isaiah is speaking of salvation as a person—Yeshua. Could this scripture be referring to modern Israel since it is addressed to "the daughter of Zion?" Would the message be, "Tell Israel, your Yeshua is coming bringing with him his reward and recompense"? Seems to be a very strong possibility! ["Recompense" defined: to give compensation for an injury or loss.]

Amos 9:14-15

I will restore the fortunes of my people Israel, and they shall rebuild the ruined cities and inhabit them... I will plant them on their land, and <u>they shall never again be plucked up</u> out of the land which I have given them, says the Lord your God.

That sounds definitive and permanent, doesn't it? God said through the prophet, Amos, that He will restore the people of Israel to their land and restore and rebuild Israel and their ruined cities. This was necessary to reverse the curse (that of being a wasteland) as prophesied in Deuteronomy 29:23. We can look at Israel today and see that God is true to His word.

34

Tel Aviv, 1920 - Rothschild Blvd.[59]

Rothschild Blvd. Towers - 2014[60]

Now, let's listen to what God says in Ezekiel.

Ezekiel 36

(1)And you son of man, prophesy to the mountains of Israel...(2) ...Because the enemy said of you, 'Aha!' and 'The

---

[59] Rothschild Boulevard, view towards the sea around 1920 Copyright © 1979, Eli Shiller. All Rights Reserverd. Low grade pictures, published with permission.
http://www.eretzy:sroe! org/~dhershkowitz/index2.html
[60] This file is licensed under the Creative Commons Attribution-Share Alike 3.0 Unported license. Accessed at:
https://commons.wikimedia.org/wiki/File:RothschildBoulevardTowersMay2014Cropped.jpg#filelinks

ancient heights have become our possession,' (3) therefore prophesy...because <u>they have made you desolate</u>, and crushed you from all sides... (5)...I speak in my hot jealousy against the rest of the nations, and all Edom, [Arab nations] <u>who gave my land to themselves</u> as a possession with wholehearted joy and utter contempt, that they might possess it and plunder it. (8) But you O mountains of Israel, shall <u>shoot forth your branches</u>, and yield your fruit to my people Israel; for they will soon come home. (9)...I will turn to you, and you shall be tilled and sown; (22)...It is not for your sake, O house of Israel, that I am about to act, <u>but for the sake of my holy name</u>, which you have profaned among the nations...(24)...I will take you from the <u>nations</u>, and gather you <u>from all the countries</u> and bring you into your own land. (25) I will sprinkle clean water upon you, and you shall be clean from all your uncleannesses... (26) A new heart I will give you, and a new spirit I will put within you...

Here God speaks through Ezekiel warning the nations who *gave His land to themselves* as a possession that they might plunder it. Let's note that the Arab nations did not take possession of the land of Israel after Judah's dispersion in 586 B.C. History reveals that this did not happen until more than 500 years after Israel's second dispersion (70 A.D.) when Mohammed's successor, Caliph Omar, captured Jerusalem in 638 A.D.[61] In this scripture, we should notice the order of events concerning Israel's regathering. God will first take them from the nations **and then** He will cleanse them and give them a new heart and spirit. Ezekiel continues, but note the end of the desolation: *(28) You shall dwell in the land which I gave to your fathers; and you shall be my people and I will be your God. (32) ...It is not for your sake that I will act, says the Lord God;* **let that be known to you***...(34) And the land that was desolate shall be tilled, instead of being the desolation that it was* **in the sight of all** *who passed by.* [This would include

---

[61] <u>Babylon in Europe,</u> by David Hathaway, Pg. 51, New Wine Press, www.newwineministries.com.uk

36

passerby, Mark Twain.] *(35)...This land that was desolate has become like the Garden of Eden... (37)...This also I will let the house of Israel ask me to do for them: to increase their men like a flock.*

In 1867, Samuel Clemens, a.k.a., Mark Twain, traveled in Israel and described the land in a book called, *Innocents Abroad*, as "a desolate country...a silent mournful expanse...hardly a tree or shrub anywhere...the hills barren and dull, the valleys unsightly deserts..." Today the land of Israel is an agricultural wonder, producing fruit and vegetables for itself and exporting to more than ninety countries.[62] Israel celebrated its 60th Anniversary as a nation on May 8, 2008. In 1900, there were about 40,000 Jews in the land of Israel.[63] The population in Israel in 1948 was about 650,000 and has grown to more than 8,000,000 in 2015.[64] It is hard to believe that anyone would doubt that God is actively fulfilling His prophetic word. Ezekiel 36:8-9 has come to fruition. But, there's more...

Jeremiah 31:35-36
Thus says the Lord, who gives the sun for light by day and the fixed order of the moon and stars for light by night, who stirs up the sea so that its waves roar – the Lord of Hosts is His Name: If this fixed order departs from before me, says the Lord, then shall the descendants of Israel cease from being a nation before me forever.

Can't we begin to see that God is serious about the descendants of Israel? The sun, moon and stars are still giving off their light and the waves of the sea are still roaring, including tsunamis, cyclones, and hurricanes! Continuing in verse 37: *"Thus says the Lord: 'If the heavens above can be measured, and the foundations of the earth below can be*

---

[62] Israel in Bible Prophecy, Gary Fisher, Lion of Judah Ministry, www.lionofjudahministry.org
[63] *Ibid*
[64] *Hope For Israel Newsletter*, Summer 2015 issue.

explored, then I will cast off all the descendants of Israel for all that they have done, says the Lord.'" The fixed order of the heavens remain. They still cannot be measured and we still cannot explore the inner parts of the earth. It seems to me that the descendants of Israel are still a part of God's plan. Note that "says the Lord" is used twice. It's like a double emphasis! He really wants us to understand this.

Joel 3:1-2

For behold in those days and at that time, when I restore the fortunes of Judah and Jerusalem, I will gather all the nations and bring them down to the valley of Jehoshaphat and I will enter into judgment with them there, on account of my people and my heritage Israel, because they have scattered them among the nations and have divided up my land,

Could be that He's dead serious! God refers to the land of Israel as 'His' land in several places in the Bible. In Deuteronomy 11:21, God says the land belongs to Israel as long as the heavens are above the earth. This land covenant is forever, as reiterated in Genesis 17:7-8; Jeremiah 7:7; and Ezekiel. 36:5. Here in Joel, He is not happy about His land being divided! In the book, Eye to Eye,[65] White House Correspondent, William Koenig, documents catastrophic events occurring in the United States since 1988 which parallel the decisions made by U. S. Presidents and the State Department to pressure Israel to divide their land. Could these parallels be coincidence or does it indicate just how serious God is? In the Bible God uses the weather, earthquakes and plagues, etc., to get the attention of people and nations who are doing what is contrary to His will and purpose. The events in Israel's Exodus from Egypt[66] and the drought in the days of Elijah[67] are some examples. Jesus says that these kinds of catastrophic events are to precede His second coming.

---

[65] Eye to Eye, William Koenig, About Him Publishing, http://www.abouthim.org; also, Koenig's International News at http://www.watch.org/
[66] Exodus Chapters 8-12
[67] I Kings Chapters 17-19

Matthew 24:6-8

And you will hear of wars and rumors of wars; see that you are not alarmed; for this must take place, but the end is not yet. For nation will rise against nation, and kingdom against kingdom, and there will be famine and earthquakes in various places: all this is but the beginnings of sufferings.

For several years now there has been so much in the news about global warming, aka, "climate change," and what is causing it. Around the world, politicians use this to consolidate power and line their pockets. Generally speaking, the blame is attributed to man's burning of fossil fuels. At least, this is believed by those who are 'supposedly' in the know. Could it be that the weather has anything to do with man's rebellion against God, or the slaughter of over 50 million babies in the womb and the selling of their body parts to so-called "research facilities?" Could it be that the weather has anything to do with the increasing persecution and hostility toward the Jewish people around the world? Could it be? Climate change? Or judgment?

In an August 2015 article entitled, *Apocalyptic Weather Around World Sign of Fulfillment of Biblical Prophecy*, *Breaking Israel News* reported :

" 'For behold, the day is coming, burning like a furnace; and all the arrogant and every evildoer will be chaff; and the day that is coming will set them ablaze,' says the LORD of hosts, 'so that it will leave them neither root nor branch.' (Malachi 3:19)"

"Extreme weather is everywhere, but perhaps nowhere more dramatically than the scorching heat recently reported over Iran, where the heat index has been as high as 164°F (73°C). Similar temperatures are being recorded in Iraq.
"Iran and Iraq are far from alone in experiencing tumultuous weather events in recent months."

The article goes on to report:

"A recent YouTube video compiling news sources of the sudden extreme weather around the world only highlights further the international apocalyptic-type weather currently taking place. News clips of deadly floods in the Midwestern US, wildfires in California and Saskatchewan, blazing temperatures in Tennessee and Indiana, clusters of earthquakes in Alaska, threatened eruptions of Mexico's Volcano of Fire and much more illustrate the unprecedented meteorological occurrences."

The article continues with a July 15, 2015, *Fox News* report...

"...on a new study that predicts that Oregon, Washington, and parts of Northern California are way overdue for an intense, margin rupture earthquake. The predicted 9.2 [earthquake] and subsequent tsunami could, according to the Federal government, cost as many as 13,000 lives in the Pacific Northwest."[68]

Warning signs seem to be everywhere, but who is paying attention? It seems to be human nature to pay attention only after the fact or after the event and only then to seek God.

The writer of Psalm 83 asks God to break His silence because God's enemies are laying plans to destroy His people. Psalm 83 could be a prophetic prayer for Israel in our day. Let's compare **Psalm 83:4** to today's news... *"They say, 'Come let us wipe them out as a nation; let the name of Israel be remembered no more!'"* This scripture could practically be taken from the charters of terrorist organizations such as Hamas and Hezbollah. The psalm goes on to list the Arab

---

[68]*Breaking Israel News, article:*
http://www.breakingisraelnews.com/46395/apocalyptic-weather-around-world-
sign-of-fulfillment-biblical-prophecy-jewish-world/#ruxyePdCB7Qw5rpO.99

nations whose descendants surround Israel today. Then the psalmist asks God to do to these enemies as He had done to previous enemies **who had said** in Verse 12, *"Let us take possession for ourselves of the pastures of God."* Isn't that what Israel's neighbors are trying to do today? Take possession of the land that God says is His?

One reliable news source reported on June 6, 2008, that the President of Iran said Israel "will soon be erased from the geographical scene,"[69] and many such threats have been made since. It has been reported that the current supreme leader of Iran, Ayatollah Ali Khameini, recently stated that, "It is the mission of the Islamic Republic of Iran to erase Israel from the map."

Zechariah 12:2-3 KJV
Behold, I will make Jerusalem a cup of trembling unto all the people round about, when they shall be in the siege both against Judah and against Jerusalem. And in that day will I make Jerusalem a burdensome stone for all people: all that burden themselves with it shall be cut in pieces, though all the people of the earth be gathered together against it.

"What to do about Jerusalem"—a dilemma for the leaders of the world who are working so feverishly to make peace happen between the Jews and Muslims. God tells us that He will make Jerusalem a cup of trembling and a burdensome stone for all people.[70] He also warns that "on that day" Jerusalem is going to be a big problem for the nations and all who try to "lift that stone" will grievously hurt themselves.[71] However, at long last, Israel will recognize and mourn for the One they have pierced, Yeshua (Jesus), their Messiah. Read on!

---

[69] Flash Traffic: Washington Update, Joel C. Rosenberg, June 6, 2008
[70] Zechariah 12:2
[71] Zechariah12:3

Zechariah 12:9-10

And on that day I will seek to destroy all the nations that come against Jerusalem. And I will pour out on the house of David and the inhabitants of Jerusalem a spirit of compassion and supplication, so that, when they look on him whom they have pierced, they shall mourn for him, as one mourns for an only child, and weep bitterly over him, as one weeps over a first-born.

Jeremiah 50:4-5

In those days and in that time, says the Lord, **the people of Israel and the people of Judah shall come together,** *weeping as they come; and they shall seek the Lord their God. They shall ask the way to Zion, with faces toward it, saying, "Come, let us join ourselves to the Lord in an everlasting covenant which will never be forgotten."*

We know who Judah is... but, who is this Israel to whom Jeremiah is referring? Could this be Ephraim? The northern kingdom whom God said that He divorced?[72]   Think about it! At no time in history have the people of Israel and of Judah ever *come* together to search for the way to Zion. Consider also, *"...Thus says the LORD God: Behold, I am about to take the stick of Joseph (which is in the hand of Ephraim) and the tribes of Israel associated with him; and I will join with it the stick of Judah, and make them one stick, that they may be one in my hand (Ezekiel 37:19)."* Read also Jeremiah 3:18. More on this later.

Jeremiah 16:14-16

Therefore, behold, the days are coming, says the Lord, **when it shall no longer be said, 'As the Lord lives who brought up the people of Israel out of the land of Egypt,' but 'As the Lord lives who brought up the people of_Israel out of the north country** *and* **out of all the countries** *where He had driven them.'* **For I will bring them back to their own land**

---

[72] Jeremiah 3:6-8

which I gave to their fathers. Behold, I am sending for many fishers, says the Lord, and they shall catch them; and afterwards I will send for many hunters and they shall hunt them from every mountain and every hill, and out of the clefts of the rocks.

Get this! The greatest miracle that Israel celebrates **will no longer be** the Exodus from Egypt----it will be the return (*aliyah*) back to Israel from all the countries where God had driven them!! He even says that He will send fishers and hunters after them. If this miracle is going to be greater than the parting of the Red Sea[73] and backing up the waters of the Jordan River at flood stage,[74] can you imagine what God has in store for Israel?

Later, in Jeremiah, God says that the LORD will raise up for David a righteous branch (Jesus) who will reign as King **and in His days,** Judah will be saved and Israel will be secure. Jeremiah continues and repeats word for word the "greater than the Exodus from Egypt" prophecy of Jeremiah 16... dual emphasis.[75]

Micah 4:1-2
It shall come to pass in the latter days...nations shall come, and say: "Come, let us go up to the mountain of the LORD, to the house of the God of Jacob; that He may teach us His ways and we may walk in His paths."

Oh, happy day!! What a day it will be when peoples and nations no longer seek their own selfish desires, but actually seek the Way of the God of Jacob—the God of Israel and discover the blessings that come with following His instructions. No longer will they make war but they will

---

[73] Exodus 14:21-22
[74] Joshua 3:15-17
[75] Jeremiah 23:5-8

actually learn to love and respect their neighbors and to know and love God!

Here are some additional prophecies concerning Israel:

One would think that the scriptural evidence already presented is more than enough to prove God's faithfulness to Israel. Below are listed numerous scriptures with a brief synopsis of each that indicate God has a plan that is ongoing for Judah and Israel. I would encourage you to read some or all of these scriptures.

Isaiah 2:2-4	**Judah and Jerusalem to be established.**
Isaiah 14:1	**God will have compassion and <u>again</u> choose Israel.**
Isaiah 41:8-10	**Israel is God's servant and not cast off.**
Isaiah 43:1-7	**Israel redeemed–gathered from North, South, East & West.**
Isaiah 44:1-5	**God to pour His Spirit on Israel.**
Isaiah 44:21-22	**Israel not to be forgotten-Sins swept away.**
Isaiah 60, 61 & 62	**Three chapters—God's prophecies for Israel.**
Jeremiah 3:12-18	**Israel's return to Zion – Judah and Israel unite.**
Jeremiah 3:22	**Israel repents. God forgives them.**
Jeremiah 50:4-5	**Judah and Israel seek an everlasting covenant with God.**
Jeremiah 12:14-17	**God to pluck up Judah then return them to the land.**
Jeremiah 23:5-8	**Righteous Branch to rule regathered Israel.**
Jeremiah 30 & 31	**God's plan negates Replacement Theology.**

Jeremiah 33:7-8	**God to restore fortunes of Judah & Israel.**
Ezekiel 11:14-20	**God restores Israel to the land and gives them a new heart and spirit.**
Ezekiel 20:33-34	**Mighty hand to gather Israel.**
Ezekiel 28:24-26	**Gathers Israel-manifests His holiness.**
Ezekiel 34:11-31	**God gathers his sheep (house of Israel) to Israel and blesses them.**
Ezekiel 36:8-37	**God restores and cleanses Israel for the sake of His Holy Name.**
Ezekiel 37	**Israel. As the old song says, "*Them bones, them bones, them dry bones!*"**
Ezekiel 37:15-23	**Judah and Israel (Joseph and Ephraim) to become one nation.**
Ezekiel 38:1-9	**Alliance of nations comes against Israel in the latter years.**
Ezekiel 38	**God will defend Israel.**
Ezekiel 39:25-29	**God restores Israel – gathers its people – leaves none among the nations.**
Joel 2:18-29	**God to have pity-Israel no more a reproach.**
Joel 3:1-2	**God restores Judah & Jerusalem-judges nations.**
Zephaniah 3:14-20	**Israel to rejoice-gathered –brought home.**
Zechariah 8:9-23	**Peace to be sowed-Israel to be a blessing-peoples & nations to seek God in Jerusalem.**
Zechariah 8:13	**God saves Israel and Judah.**
Zechariah 9:16-17	**God saves His people-they shine like jewels on His land.**
Zechariah 10:6-12	**God gathers, redeems Judah and Joseph (Israel).**
Zechariah 12	**Victory for Judah and Jerusalem!**
Zechariah 14	**Jesus returns to the Mount of Olives.**

| **Hosea 3:4-5** | **Israel will live a long time without a king, then come to the Lord in the latter days.** |

And there are many more!   With all these scriptural references regarding God's plan and purpose for Israel, shouldn't we come to the conclusion that there could be consequences to avoiding the Truth of His Word?   When something is true and by our actions we avoid or ignore that truth we should be prepared for an unwelcome consequence, a consequence that seems all the more real and inevitable as the days go by and "that day" draws near.

God's covenant with, and His promises for the children of Israel are on a firm foundation according to the prophets of old. Next, we'll look at the New Testament and the first century Church.   Who were they? And just what was the foundation of their theology?

$$\ast\ast\ast\ast$$

A personal note…

The mid 1960s was a time in my life that was quite eventful. I graduated from Texas A&M in 1965, taught school and coached several sports for a year in a small Texas community and, in the fall of 1966, was obligated to serve out my commission as an officer in the United States Army Signal Corps. Prior to my military departure, I was visiting home on a weekend.   My younger brother, Larry, was also home that weekend. I can't remember what day it was… Larry tells me that it was a Sunday morning and we were skipping church even though Mom had encouraged us to go.

We walked out of the house and, much to our surprise, saw a flock of turkeys about a hundred yards down our driveway. Seeing a flock of wild turkeys was a rare occurrence and being raised as hunters in the Texas Hill Country, we really got excited! We hurried back into the house and grabbed a couple of .22 caliber rifles... then, hopped into my "new-to-me" '64 Ford Galaxy 500 XL two-door hardtop and headed down the driveway. By that time the turkeys had gone down into a nearby creek bottom. So, Larry got out of the car and proceeded after them. It was my bright idea to take the car out to the highway and drive around to the other side of the turkeys. I did just that and we had them surrounded!

I got out of the car and walked up a small embankment. That's when I heard Larry shoot and, about that same time, I heard a bullet whizzing by. It was kind of like the ricochet sound in old western movies. I thought I'd better get out of there pronto, but just as I turned, another shot sounded and at about the same time something hit me in the neck! The impact knocked me to my knees. It didn't take long for me to realize that I could be in serious trouble. I placed my hand over the wound to suppress the bleeding and yelled for Larry to come quick. When I told him that I had been hit, I thought he was going to pass out.

We gathered our wits, got into that white Ford and headed for the nearest hospital/clinic, which was fifteen miles away in Johnson City. I think Larry was more afraid than I was because he kept asking me if I was OK. I never removed my hand from the wound and answered, "Yeah, I'm OK." He must have used most of the 390 cubic inches under the hood of that "new-to-me" Ford as we arrived at the clinic in about ten minutes. Fortunately, there was a doctor at the clinic when we arrived. He removed the .22 caliber slug, cleaned and bandaged the wound and we were in and out of the clinic in about an hour. The slug missed my carotid artery by about an inch and stopped just short of the vertebrae in my neck by about a half-inch. The first possibility would have meant bleeding to death before we could get to the hospital and the second possibility... paralysis. Now, why am I telling you this? My brother Larry and I had both hunted for years prior to that incident and had been taught by our dad the need to respect and adhere to certain truths about proper hunting rules. We had violated those truths and I suffered the consequences. They could have been much worse!

Larry told me Mom never cooked the "other" turkey he bagged that day! I don't really remember because I was soon off to Georgia and New Jersey for Signal Corps training and from there to South Korea. Oh, and that white Ford? It was one of my most prized possessions for twenty years! It's kind of crazy how possessions can become so important to us. But when it gets down to the nuts and bolts of life, they are truly insignificant.

CHAPTER FOUR

THE NEW TESTAMENT

The evidence of Old Testament scripture clearly says that God is emphatic about His prerecorded plan for the people and the land of Israel. But what does the New Testament say? In my view, the New Testament is the promise of a "renewed covenant" that is still in the process of being made complete.

The writer of Hebrews, quoting Jeremiah 31:31, explains that if God's first covenant with Israel had found the people without fault, there would be no need for a second covenant. *"'The days will come' says the Lord, 'when I will establish a new covenant with the **house of Israel** and with the **house of Judah**; not like the covenant that I made with their fathers... I will put my laws into their minds and write them on their hearts...(Hebrews 8:7-10).'"* This is New Testament scripture using the Old Testament to verify that God still has a plan for Judah and Israel. This scripture clearly is NOT speaking about the Church. Just who is the New Covenant with?

The first Christian church was entirely Jewish. On the day of Pentecost, following the resurrection, the disciples of Jesus were gathered in one place when the Holy Spirit showed up. The Holy Spirit was described as a mighty rushing wind.[76] Pentecost is the same day referred to in Hebrew as *Shavuot,* which was the culmination of the Feast of Weeks—7 weeks— a 49 day counting period to the 50th day. *Pentekostos,* from where the word Pentecost comes, is the Greek word for 50. *Shavuot* (Pentecost) is the celebration of the day that God's Law was given at Mt. Sinai, and is one of three festivals, which God ordained for all Israel and has been kept by the Jewish

---

[76] Acts 2:1-2

49

people since the very first Passover in Egypt. They still keep it. Jews were commanded to make a pilgrimage to Jerusalem for the Feasts of Passover, Pentecost, and Tabernacles.[77] Literally thousands of people made these pilgrimages to Jerusalem each year.

On that Day of Pentecost, in addition to the local Jews, there were devout Jews from 15 different nations who spoke different languages and who had made that pilgrimage to Jerusalem. This crowd was astonished at being able to understand the apostles because they knew the apostles were Galileans. And yet they heard the Gospel in their own languages.[78] Then Peter stood and addressed the crowd: *"Men of Israel, hear these words: Jesus of Nazareth...this Jesus, delivered up* **according to the definite plan and foreknowledge of God***, you crucified and killed by the hands of lawless men.* [Did you catch that? Jesus was delivered up according to God's plan!] *But God raised Him up, having loosed the pangs of death, because it was not possible for him to be held by it* (Acts 2:22-24)." *"Let all the house of Israel therefore know assuredly that God has made him both Lord and Christ, this Jesus whom you crucified (Acts 2:36)!"* The crowd of Jews was convicted by Peter's message and then asked what were they to do? Peter told them *"Repent, and be baptized every one of you in the name of Jesus Christ for the forgiveness of your sins (Acts 2:37-38)..."* We're then told in verse 41 that 3000 received the word and were baptized, which just happens to be exactly the same number of souls that perished due to the worship of the golden calf at Mt. Sinai! God is a God of Justice, so is this just a coincidence?

Paul and Jesus' disciples were all Jewish. Some say Luke, the writer of the Gospel, may not have been Jewish. Noted author and co-author of more than ten books on Bible prophecy

---

[77] The Complete Jewish Bible, Glossary, *Shavuot*, Page 1591, David H. Stern, Jewish New Testament Publications, Inc.
[78] Acts 2:5-12

50

and former teacher at Dallas Baptist University and Dallas Bible College, Dr. Thomas S. McCall, points out that Luke was very knowledgeable about the Temple and Gentiles were not allowed in the Temple. Dr. McCall says, "…we must infer that Luke was a Jew."[79] Therefore, it is questionable that he was a Gentile.

The Jews were entrusted with the very words of God… *"To begin with, the Jews are entrusted with the oracles of God* (Romans 3:2)." There would not be a Bible if it weren't for the Jewish people. The fact that you and I can read and treasure the word of the God of Abraham, Isaac and Jacob is a result of faithful Hebrew scribes and the Jews who were entrusted with the Oracles of God making certain that God's word was preserved for future generations.

We should also remember that the disciples of Jesus did not have a "New Testament," but only had the Torah, The Prophets, and The Writings of the Old Testament, which is referred to in Hebrew as the 'Tanakh.' Every time that they referred to a scripture, it would have been to these writings. Yeshua and His disciples **only used Old Testament scriptures**. One example would be, in Matthew Chapter 4, Yeshua quoted a portion of Deuteronomy 8:3. *"…It is written, 'man shall not live by bread alone, but by every word that proceeds from the mouth of God.'* (Matthew 4:4)." *"…that He might make you know that man does not live by bread alone, but that man lives by everything that proceeds out of the mouth of the LORD* (Deuteronomy 8:3)." Note that the New Testament was not canonized until late in the third century. **Christianity based solely on the New Testament is without a foundation.**

Within about a hundred years or so after the death of the Apostle Paul and the disciples, Gentile leaders began to have

---

[79] Lamplighter, September/October 2007, *Was Luke a Gentile,* by Dr. Thomas S. McCall

greater influence on the direction of the Church. They sought to distance themselves from anything they considered Jewish, and in general, began to allegorize the Old Testament in order to justify their theology. Of repute was a man named Marcion, a theologian in the second half of the second century, who taught that there was such a separation between law and grace that the two were not representative of the same God... thus, two gods![80] His teachings were rejected as heresies by the Church; however, the "ghost" of Marcion is alive even today.

Regrettably, allegorizing and twisting of Old Testament scriptures is prevalent in much of Christianity today, i.e., "the Old Testament and the Law is only for the Jews while the New Testament and the understanding of the Law presented there is applicable to the Church," but somehow, not the same as the Law delivered at Mt. Sinai. If one is to follow this theology, is it not to say that the God of the Old Testament is somehow not the same God that Jesus referred to when He said, *"I and the Father are one (John 10:30)?"* Following this theology, one might be following a "Jesus" who is not reflective of the Jesus who is portrayed and identified as the Savior of the world by the prophets of the Old Testament. Those prophets very accurately prophesied His coming, His death, burial and resurrection, all of which were fulfilled and recorded in the New Testament. Jesus said, *"Think not that I have come to abolish the law and the prophets; I have come not to abolish them but to fulfill them (Matthew 5:17)."* If He didn't come to abolish the Law, it stands to reason that it still has relevance. He continues, *"I tell you the truth, until heaven and earth disappears, not the smallest letter, not the least stroke of a pen, will by any means disappear from the Law until everything is accomplished (Matthew 5:18 NIV)."* Both testaments, the "old" and the "new," are essential for our understanding. The truth of one supports the truth of the other.

---

[80] *"The Ghost of Marcion: What Paul's Letters Really Say,"* http://www.MessianicPublications.Com/daniel-botkin/the-ghost-of-marcion/ - Accessed 9-21-15

There have been many times that I have heard it expressed that it is impossible to keep all 613 commandments. I don't know how many there are, I've never counted them, but I would agree that you can't keep them all. Some of the commandments only pertain to the temple in Jerusalem, which at this time does not exist. And some only apply if you are physically in the land of Israel. Some pertain to kings, priests, judges, men, women, and children, and are applicable only if you fit in one of these categories. Yeshua/Jesus, our Passover Lamb, was the once and for all sacrifice for sin,[81] so God's just requirement for the sacrifice for sin is complete. However, as you continue to read, you will find that God's Law still applies. I acknowledge that I do not understand the "why" of every law in the Old Testament, but I trust that God has a reason for every word He has spoken or inspired. The reason is obvious for some laws, and not so obvious for others, but the reason for all is to accomplish His purpose for establishing justice and righteousness in all the earth.

His laws are not nearly so numerous and burdensome as they are made out to be... In fact, according to scripture, they are not a burden at all! *"For this commandment which I command you this day is not too hard for you, neither is it far off* (Deuteronomy 30:11). " And, *"For this is the love of God, that we keep His commandments. And His commandments are not burdensome* (1 John 5:3). " Many Christians today consider God's Law to be bondage. That is what the Church has taught but it is not true according to scripture! *"But he who looks into the **perfect law, the law of liberty,** and perseveres, being no hearer that forgets but a doer that acts, he shall be blessed in his doing* (James 1:25). " The *"perfect law of liberty"* are the words of James, the brother of Jesus! Where do we get the idea that the Law is a burden? It is not in scripture!

---

[81] Hebrews 10:10

I'd like to point out here that we have one God and one Word. God is not divided and He is One from the beginning to the end. The Old and New Testaments do not divide the word of God. They are one from Genesis to Revelation and the truth of one supports and verifies the truth of the other and neither is intended to stand alone.

We'll see an example of the bridge, or connection, between the Old and New Testaments in our study in the next chapter. There we will learn that God had a plan that included Gentiles as well as the children of Israel. What we find may come as a bit of a surprise!

Perhaps you noticed the menorah and cross design on the dedication page in the front of this book. Basically, it's the vision I was given when LaVada and I recorded our very first CD project, *In God's Time* (not a literal vision — but, I don't know how I could otherwise explain where it came from). For us, it seems to illustrate Christians getting back to 'the Jewish or Hebrew roots' of Christianity.

The menorah design was given by God to Moses.[82] The middle branch of the menorah is referred to in Hebrew as "Shamash" (the servant) and "Ner Elohim" (the lamp of God). An interesting side note here is that if we place the first seven Hebrew words of the Torah (Genesis 1:1) over a menorah, it looks like this. [83]

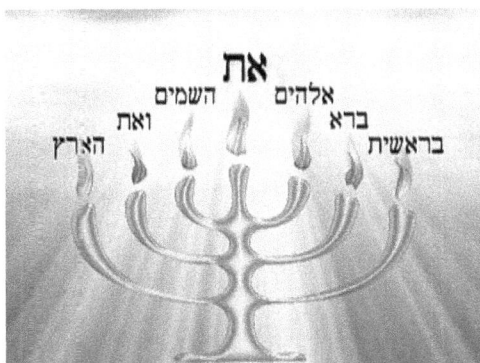

Hebrew is written and read from right to left. Thus, the Hebrew reads, "BERESHIT BARAH ELOHIM

[82] Exodus 25:31-40
[83] Jewish Jewels, January 2006 Newsletter; http://www.jewishjewels.org/newsletters/2006_01.htm, accessed 11-24-2008

ET (את) HASHAMAYIM VAYET HA ERETZ." Note the Alef and the Tav את over the servant candle. This is not coincidence! It simply indicates God's hand in every detail of His word. In the beginning Elohim—God—Yeshua—the Alef and the Tav (Alpha and Omega) created the heavens and the earth.

In the first seven words of the Bible, God records his servant Yeshua, the Alef and Tav, in the midst of the creation account. *"He is the image of the invisible God, the firstborn of all creation; for in Him all things were created in heaven and on earth, visible and invisible, whether thrones or dominions or principalities or authorities—all things were created through Him and for Him* (Colossians 1:15-16)."

CHAPTER FIVE
THE NEW TESTAMENT AND PAUL'S TEACHING

The Apostle Paul is possibly the most misunderstood writer in the New Testament. He was accused again and again of teaching against Torah/Law by various Jewish contemporaries. Ironically, many Christians today accuse him of teaching the same thing. Peter warned believers in his day that Paul was hard to understand and that, even then, there were those who twisted his teachings.

> *"And count the forbearance of our Lord as salvation. So also our beloved brother Paul wrote to you according to the wisdom given him speaking of this as he does in all his letters. There are some things in them **hard to understand**, which the ignorant and unstable twist to their own destruction, as they do the other scriptures."[84]*

In Acts 24, Paul was on trial and had been accused of being a rabble-rouser and a ringleader of the "Nazarenes." He defended himself by saying that it hadn't been more than twelve days since he had been to worship in Jerusalem and that no one had found him stirring up a crowd in the temple, the synagogues or in the city. In Acts 24:14, he says, *"But this I do admit to you: I worship the God of our fathers in accordance with the Way, which they call a sect. [Sect of Judaism!] I continue to believe everything that accords with the Torah [the Law] and everything written in the Prophets."[85]*

---

[84] 2 Peter 3:15-16

[85] Acts 24:14 <u>The Complete Jewish Bible,</u> David H. Stern, Jewish New Testament Publications, Inc.

I'll cover more of Paul's teaching on the Law in Chapter Six, but for now, let's examine the Old Testament relationship between Gentiles and the nation of Israel. The idea of Gentiles being grafted into God's people, Israel, as expressed by Paul in Roman's Chapter 11, which we'll discuss shortly, was not a new concept. The Book of Acts records that the apostle, James, related that God would take out of the Gentiles a people for His name and that the word of the prophets agreed with this concept.[86] This idea is recorded in the writings of Moses, as well, most notably expressed in Israel's exodus from Egypt, where it is recorded that a *mixed multitude* (perhaps thousands, or even a hundred thousand or more) joined the exodus. This "mixed multitude" is translated from the Hebrew word, *ereb,* which translates as foreign people, mixed people, aliens or Gentiles. (Strong's H6154) Foreigners were generally contrasted with the "native Israelites," 'native' from the Hebrew word, *ezrach,* (H249) means native, born in the land, [or] of one's own country [or nation, or people].[87] In this case, the Israelites were those people descended from Jacob, or Israel, who were not yet in "the land of Israel."

The English translation of the Old Testament scriptures is sometimes a bit confusing when it speaks of these foreign people, at times in a positive light, and at other times, negatively. The reason... the Hebrew words *ger* (H1616) and *nokriy* (H5237) were **both** translated as "foreigner, alien, stranger, or sojourner." Simply stated, there were two kinds of these foreigners or strangers, etc. One was referred to positively (*ger*) and one was referred to negatively (*nokriy*). A positive referral meant that the *ger* had joined themselves to Israel and would follow the statutes and laws of Israel. The *nokriy*, or negative referral, did not follow God's laws.[88]

---

[86] Acts 15:15
[87] David Ben Yisrael, *The Mixed Multitude* video, http://www.setapartmountain.com
[88] *Ibid.*

There are many examples of these terms used throughout scripture. I will quote a few.

For the "positive" *ger*:

Exodus 12:49
There shall be one law for the native [ezrach] *and for the stranger* [ger] *who sojourns among you.*

Exodus 20:10
...but the seventh day is a sabbath to the LORD your God; in it you shall not do any work, you, or your son, or your daughter, your manservant, or your maidservant, or your cattle, **or the sojourner [ger] who is within your gates;**

Leviticus 19:34
The stranger [ger] *who sojourns with you shall be to you as the native* [ezrach] *among you, and you shall love him as yourself...*

Let's note that there was to be one Law for both the stranger and the native. Isaiah records that there is a positive future for the *ger*.

Isaiah 14:1
The LORD will have compassion on Jacob and will again choose Israel, and will set them in their own land, and aliens [ger] *will join them and will cleave to the house of Jacob.*

For the "negative" *nokriy*:

1 Kings 11:8-9
[Referring to Solomon] *And so he did for all his foreign* [nokriy] *wives, who burned incense and sacrifice to their gods. And the LORD was angry with Solomon...*

Jeremiah 2:21-22 KJV
Yet I had planted thee a noble vine, wholly a right seed: how then art thou turned into the degenerate plant of a strange [nokriy] vine unto me? ... yet thine iniquity [sin, lawlessness] is marked before me, saith the Lord GOD.

Deuteronomy 23:20
To a foreigner [nokriy] you may lend upon interest, but to your brother you shall not lend upon interest...

From these scriptures we can ascertain that the *nokriy* served other gods and by doing so did not honor the God of Israel. They were not to be treated as brothers.

So now we see that the concept of Gentiles (*ger*) being "grafted in" was practiced in the time of Moses because it was commanded.[89] Gentiles were to be accepted, so long as they kept God's Law, and were to be loved just as the native Israelites. Consider that Naomi's daughter-in-law, Ruth, a Gentile, was the great grandmother of King David,[90] thus, she was in the lineage of the Messiah. There is not a better way to illustrate what it means to be "grafted in" than the well-known passage in Ruth... *"Don't urge me to leave you or to turn back from you. Where you go I will go, and where you stay I will stay. Your people will be my people and your God my God. Where you die I will die, and there I will be buried. May the LORD deal with me, be it ever so severely, if anything but death separates you and me (Ruth 1:16-17NIV)."*

Now, let's focus on Paul's teaching about his Jewish kinsmen and their relationship to Gentiles. He refers to Isaiah 65:2 in **Romans 10:21,** *All day long I stretch my hand to a contrary and disobedient Israel.*

---

[89] Leviticus 19:34
[90] Ruth 4:17

Romans 9:1-3

I am speaking the truth in Christ, I am not lying; my conscience bears me witness in the Holy Spirit, that I have great sorrow and unceasing anguish in my heart. For I could wish that I myself were accursed and cut off from Christ for the sake of my brethren, my kinsmen by race.

Paul was very troubled about his kinsmen. In the very first verse of Romans 11, Paul asked the question "Has God rejected Israel?" No hesitation here—his answer was point-blank, "By no means!" In other words, "No way!" Apparently, some folks even in his day were saying that God no longer had a plan or use for the Jewish people! Let's take a look at what he says in Chapter 11.

Summary of Romans 11:

1 - Has God rejected Israel? ***BY NO MEANS...***

2 - **God has not rejected** *His people whom He foreknew.*

7 - What then? Israel failed to obtain what it sought. The elect obtained it but the rest were hardened,

11 - ...through their trespass, salvation has come to the Gentiles, so as to make Israel jealous.

12 - Now if their trespass means riches for the world, and if their failure means riches for the Gentile, how much more will their full inclusion mean!

15 - For if their rejection means the reconciliation of the world, what will their acceptance mean but life from the dead?

16 - ...if the root is holy, so are the branches.

17-18 - But if some of the branches were broken off and you a wild olive shoot, were grafted in their place to share the richness of the olive tree, do not boast over the branches...remember that it is not you that supports the root, but the root that supports you. [Notice the warning!!]

Here, Paul says Gentile believers are grafted in as a "wild olive shoot." This teaching is based in part on the words recorded by Jeremiah. Judah, the Southern Kingdom, and Israel, the Northern Kingdom, are referred to as a "green olive tree" in Jeremiah 11:16-17... *"The Lord once called you, 'a green olive tree, fair with goodly fruit;' but with the roar of a great tempest he will set fire to it, and its branches will be consumed. The Lord of Hosts, who planted you, has pronounced evil against you, because of the evil which the house of Israel and the house of Judah have done, provoking me to anger by burning incense to Ba'al."*

19 - You will say, 'branches were broken off so that I might be grafted in.'
20 - That is true. ...do not become proud but stand in awe. [Note the admonition.]
21 - For if God did not spare the natural branches neither will He spare you. [Again, the warning.]
*22 - Note...God's kindness to you, **provided** you continue in His kindness; otherwise you too will be cut off.* [Another warning!!]
*23 - ...**God has the power to graft them** in again* [Israel and Judah] ...
*25 - ...**understand this mystery**, brethren: a hardening has come upon part of Israel, **until the full number of Gentiles come in**.*

Here Paul's comment on the Gentiles parallels Jesus/Yeshua's words in Luke 21:24..."*Jerusalem will be trodden down by the Gentiles, until the times of the Gentiles are fulfilled.*"

*26 - ...**all Israel will be saved.***
*27 - "And this will be my covenant with them **when I take away their sins.***"

28 - As regards the gospel they are enemies of God, for your sake; but as regards election they are beloved for the sake of their forefathers.
*29 - **For the gifts and the call of God are irrevocable.***
31 - ...by the mercy shown to you they also may receive mercy.
*32 - **For God has designed all men for disobedience, that He may have mercy upon all.***

We should note here the timing of when all Israel is to be saved—**when the full number of Gentiles comes into Israel** and **when God takes away their sins.** Paul refers to this as a mystery. He is speaking specifically to Gentile believers whom he says are grafted into Israel. Please take note that his admonitions and warnings, again, are directed to **Gentiles**! He says pretty much the same thing to the Gentiles in Ephesus, where he tells them that they had been *"alienated from the commonwealth of Israel, and strangers to the covenants of promise, having no hope and without God in the world. But now in Christ Jesus you who were once afar off have been brought near by the blood of Christ (Ephesians 2:12-13)."* Note that he says "covenants" of promise indicating more than one.

Paul is emphatic about God's plan for Israel as emphasized in Jeremiah 31 and many other prophetic scriptures.

Jeremiah 31:31-37 (NIV)

"The time is coming," declares the LORD, "when I will make a new covenant with the house of Israel and with the house of Judah. It will not be like the covenant I made with their forefathers when I took them by the hand to lead them out of Egypt, because they broke my covenant, though I was a husband to them, " declares the LORD. "This is the covenant I will make with the house of Israel after that time," declares the LORD. "I will put my law in their minds and write it on their

hearts. I will be their God, and they will be my people. No longer will a man teach his neighbor, or a man his brother, saying, 'Know the LORD,' because they will all know me, from the least of them to the greatest," declares the LORD. "For I will forgive their wickedness and will remember their sins no more." This is what the LORD says, he who appoints the sun to shine by day, who decrees the moon and stars to shine by night, who stirs up the sea so that its waves roar-- the LORD Almighty is his name: "Only if these decrees vanish from my sight," declares the LORD, "will the descendants of Israel ever cease to be a nation before me." This is what the LORD says: "Only if the heavens above can be measured and the foundations of the earth below be searched out will I reject all the descendants of Israel because of all they have done," declares the LORD."

Only if— will I reject the descendants of Israel. The prophet Jeremiah prophesies of a day when all will know the LORD. There will be no need for a teacher, preacher, or evangelist. God's Law will be in the minds and written on the hearts of all. This is yet to come! But for now preachers are still preaching, "Know the LORD!" and it is obvious that it is still needed.

In Romans 11:29, Paul was reminding us that God's covenant with Abraham, Isaac and Jacob about two thousand years prior, was irrevocable and would still be in effect some two thousand years later. His letter to the Romans is pointing out that God's purpose will stand and that God is not a man who would go about changing his mind. In other words, *"the gifts and call of God"* are relevant today and are still *"irrevocable."*

As I mentioned at the beginning of this chapter, Paul was accused of teaching against the Torah/Law. In the next chapter we'll look to see if there is a basis for this accusation.

CHAPTER SIX

WHICH LAW, PAUL?

As I stated in the Foreword, the primary focus of this book is to emphasize the scriptural basis for Israel's right to the land of Israel and to expose the error in the anti-Semitic teachings of the Church. At the root of the divide between Jews and Christians is the Christian lack of understanding and practice of God's Law, which has been handed down through the teachings and traditions of the Church. Because of and across this divide, there is separation, which often results in enmity. Much of the discord between Jews and Christians with regard to the Messiah is attributable to the Christian understanding of Paul's writings and their inclination to minimize the importance of the Old Testament. As pointed out earlier, Paul's writings were and are hard to understand; Paul has been accused of teaching against the Torah/Law.

Let's examine some of Paul's teachings on the Law and see what is so confusing. Before we do that, perhaps we should define the word, "sin." *"Whosoever committeth sin transgresseth also the law; for sin is the transgression of the law* (1 John 3:4 KJV)." In other words, to sin is to miss the mark in following God's instructions. If there is no Law, then it stands to reason that there would be no such thing as sin. Luther made a statement that said much the same, "I wonder exceedingly how it came to be imputed to me that I should reject the law of Ten Commandments...whoever abrogates the law must of necessity abrogate sin also."—*Martin Luther*, Spiritual Antichrist, *Pgs. 71 & 72.*

Ephesians 2:11-12
Therefore remember that at one time you Gentiles in the flesh, called the uncircumcision by what is called the circumcision, which is made in the flesh by hand—remember

that you were at that time separated from Christ, alienated from the commonwealth of Israel and strangers to the covenants of promise, having no hope and without God in the world.

As I pointed out earlier Paul's reference to the covenants of promise is plural. Undoubtedly, he is referring to both the Abrahamic (faith) and the Sinai (Law) covenants. Paul tells us, *"For the gifts and call of God are irrevocable* (Romans 11:29)." Thus, we can be assured that God's covenants and promise are valid today. *"...the law, which came 430 years afterward, does not annul a covenant previously ratified by God, so as to make the promise void* (Galatians 3:17)."

Now, bear with me for a while. We're trying to understand Paul—remember?

Paul continues...

Ephesians 2:14-16
*For He is our peace, who has made us both one, and has broken down the dividing wall of hostility, **by abolishing in His flesh the law of commandments and ordinances**, that He might create in Himself one new man in place of the two, so making peace, and might reconcile us both to God in one body through the cross, and thereby bringing the hostility to an end.*

Galatians 2:15-16
*We ourselves, who are Jews by birth and not Gentile sinners, yet who know that a man is not justified by works of the law but through faith in Jesus Christ, even we have believed in Christ Jesus, in order to be justified by faith in Christ, and not by works of the law, because **by works of the law shall no one be justified**.*

Galatians 3:13
__Christ redeemed us from the curse of the law__, having become a curse for us—for it is written, 'Cursed be everyone who hangs on a tree...

Romans 10:4
For __Christ is the end of the law__, that everyone who has faith may be justified.

Using the scriptures just quoted, we may well conclude that God's Law is no more. These scriptures and others are used by those who say that Christ fulfilled the Law, thus, the Law is not applicable today. (Note: In the scripture just quoted from Romans 10:4, the word "end" is translated from the Greek word, "telos," which can also be translated as "goal," or, "to set out for a definite point." When you put it in context with other scriptures, this translation of the word would make more sense.) Restated, it would look like this: *"For Christ is the goal of the law, that everyone who has faith may be justified."*

Let's continue with Paul's writings that seem to counter those just quoted, and compare.

Galatians 3:19
Why then the law? It was added because of transgressions, til the offspring should come to whom the promise had been made;

Romans 3:31
Do we then overthrow the law by this faith? By no means! On the contrary, __we uphold the law__.

Question: If the Law is "fulfilled" and no longer binding, why should we uphold it?

Romans 6:1-2

What shall we say then? Are we to continue in sin that grace may abound? By no means! How can we who died to sin still live in it?

Question: How could we die or live in sin, if there is no such thing as sin because there is no Law to break?

Romans 6:6

We know that our old self was crucified with Him so that the sinful body might be destroyed, and we might no longer be enslaved to sin.

Question: How can we be slaves to sin, if the Law no longer applies?

Romans 7:7

What then shall we say? That the law is sin? By no means! Yet, if it had not been for the law, I should not have known sin...

Paul hit the nail on the head here. This pretty much sums it up! If not for the Law, we wouldn't know sin. The Law is to teach and train us in righteousness and to lead us to obedience.[91]

Romans 7:12

So the law is holy, and the commandment is holy and just and good.

Do you see the problem of what appears to be contradictions in Paul's writings? Is Paul schizophrenic? I don't think so! As Peter says, Paul is hard to understand. Paul is clear that no one is justified by the Law as stated in Galatians 3:11. The Law was never given as a means to or a way to

---

[91] 2 Timothy 3:16

68

work out our salvation! But was given to be our teacher, or trainer. See 2 Timothy 3:16. What makes Paul so hard to understand is that he refers to more than one law within the Torah, which makes it difficult to identify which law Paul is referring to in numerous instances. We need to consider context as well; that is, we should consider text before and after the text being considered. Chapters and verses are for reference only, and were not in the original texts from Genesis to Revelation!

Since he refers to more than one law in his writings, knowing which law is crucial to our understanding. He references seven laws.

1. The law of God (Romans 3:31; 7:22-25; 8:7)
2. The law of sin (Romans 7:23-25)
3. The law of sin and death (Romans 8:2)
4. The law of the spirit of life (Romans 8:2)
5. The law of faith (Romans 3:27)
6. The law of righteousness (Romans 9:31)
7. The law of Christ (1 Corinthians 9:21)

I obtained the above list from 119 Ministries (testeverything.net) and their teaching series, *Which Law, Paul?* Their website is an excellent source for analysis and study of the scriptures!

Scripture tells us that the Law is spiritual[92] and the Law is Truth.[93] Paul grew up studying the Old Testament scriptures under the teacher, Gamaliel.[94] He was a scholar and was zealous for the Law. While on his way to Damascus to persecute believers he saw a great light, fell to the ground, and was struck blind.[95] Subsequently, the scales were removed

---

[92] Romans 7:14
[93] Psalm 119:142
[94] Acts 22:3
[95] Acts 9:3-4

from his eyes and he was transformed into a believer and follower of Yeshua. Once he had this encounter with Yeshua, he understood the proper application of the Torah, which he knew so well.

Ok, so let's continue with Paul's witness.

Romans 6:15-18
What then? Are we to sin because we are not under law but under grace? By no means! Do you not know that if you yield yourself to anyone as obedient slaves, you are slaves of the one whom you obey either of sin, which leads to death, or of obedience, which leads to righteousness? But thanks be to God, that you who were once slaves of sin have become obedient from the heart to the standard of teaching to which you were committed, and having been set free from sin, have become slaves of righteousness.

Romans 8:7-9
For the mind that is set on the flesh is hostile to God; it does not submit to God's law, indeed it cannot; and those who are in the flesh cannot please God. But you are not in the flesh, you are in the Spirit, if the Spirit of God really dwells in you. **Anyone who does not have the Spirit of Christ does not belong to Him.**

Romans 8:3-4
For God has done what the law, weakened by the flesh, could not do: Sending his own Son in the likeness of sinful flesh and for sin, He condemned sin in the flesh, in order that the just requirement of the law might be fulfilled in us, **who walk not according to the flesh but according to the Spirit.**

Galatians 5:18
But if you are led by the Spirit you are not under the law.

Is this beginning to make sense? If we walk according to the Spirit, which is to walk as Yeshua walked, the law of sin and death has no power over us!!

The Apostle John tells us, *"And by this we may be sure we know Him, if we keep His commandments. He who says, 'I know Him' but disobeys His commandments is a liar, and the truth is not in him. But whoever keeps His word, in him truly* **love for God is perfected**. *By this we may be sure that we are in Him: he who says he abides in Him ought to walk in the same way in which He walked* (1 John 2:3-6). " John tells us that we are to *keep His commandments* and tells us how we are to know Him.

An important meeting, known as the Council of Jerusalem, is recorded in the 15th chapter of Acts. Scripture tells us that Peter and James, as well as Paul and Barnabas, were there. And James tells us, *"But he who looks into the perfect law, the law of liberty, and perseveres, being no hearer that forgets but a doer that acts, he shall be blessed in his doing* (James 1:25). " Was there collaboration between James and Paul where they came to agreement or did they receive individual revelation? *"For it is not the hearers of the law who are righteous before God, but the doers of the law who will be justified* (Romans 2:13). "

The letter to the Hebrews is also difficult to understand, and it is possible, perhaps probable, that Paul was the writer of this letter, as well. Since Paul was an apostle sent to the Gentiles, many might disagree that he was the author of Hebrews. There were many Hebrews in the dispersion at that time and this letter was addressed to them. Scripture tells us that Paul spoke the Hebrew language.[96]

---

[96] Acts 21:40 and 26:14

The author of Hebrews writes:

Hebrews 6:17-20
So when God desired to show more convincingly to the heirs of the promise the unchangeable character of his purpose, he interposed with an oath, so that through two unchangeable things, in which it is impossible that God should prove false, we who have fled for refuge might have strong encouragement to seize the hope set before us. We have this as a sure and steadfast anchor of the soul, a hope that enters into the inner shrine behind the curtain, where Jesus has gone as a forerunner on our behalf, having become a high priest forever after the Order of Melchizedec.

The writer of Hebrews continues and later tells us that there is a change in the Law but, again, it is important to understand which law. It is not an abolition of the Torah, the first five books of our Hebrew scriptures (Old Testament), but a change of a law inside the Torah, namely, **the law of the priesthood.**

Hebrews 7:11-12
Now if perfection had been attainable through the Levitical Priesthood (for under it the people received the law), what further need would there have been for another priest to arrive after the Order of Melchizedec, rather than one named after the Order of Aaron? ***For when there is a change in the priesthood, there is necessarily a change in the law as well.***

Scriptural evidence here clearly says that the law that was changed was the law of the priesthood... not the Law, i.e., Torah. This verse is used by many to say that the Law has been done away with, contrary to what scripture clearly teaches.

Hebrews 7:15-19

This becomes even more evident when another priest arises in the likeness of Melchizedec, who has become a priest, not according to a legal requirement concerning bodily descent but by the power of an indestructible life. For it is witnessed of him, 'thou art a priest forever, after the Order of Melchizedec.' On the one hand, a former commandment is set aside because of its weakness and uselessness (for the law made nothing perfect); on the other hand, a better hope is introduced, through which we draw near to God.

Note that "a former commandment" not "commandments" is set aside. The former commandment that was set aside was set aside because of its weakness and uselessness, for that law made nothing perfect. Which law? Just back up to verse 11 for the answer. If perfection had been attained through the Levitical priesthood, specifically the High Priest, why would there be a need for another priest?

Hebrews 8:8, 10

*For he **finds fault with them** when he says: 'The days will come, says the Lord, when I will establish a new covenant with the House of Israel and with the House of Judah; ...This is the covenant that I will make with the House of Israel after those days, says the Lord: I will put my laws into their minds, and write them on their hearts, and I will be their God, and they shall be my people.* This is a quote from Jeremiah 31:31 as previously quoted.

God did not make a mistake when He gave the Law at Mt. Sinai. Note that He *"finds fault with **them**,"* i.e. **the people of Israel, not the Law.** How would He remedy this problem? He would take His Law from stone and place into their minds and their hearts.

Hebrews 8:13

In speaking of a new covenant he treats the first as obsolete. And what is becoming obsolete and growing old is ready to vanish away.

Why wouldn't a covenant written on stone be obsolete as compared to one written on our hearts and minds by the eternal heavenly priest, Yeshua/Jesus?? When Jesus gave up His Spirit on the cross, the veil that separated the most holy place in the temple was torn from top to bottom indicating a change in the priesthood.[97] This points us to the hope we have for direct access to the inner shrine where Jesus went as a forerunner on our behalf,[98] a better hope through which we draw near to God.[99] Yeshua was a one-time Passover sacrifice for sin, not a sacrifice that needed to be repeated year after year.

Hebrews 9:25-26, 28

Nor was it to offer Himself repeatedly, as the high priest enters the Holy Place yearly with blood not his own;for then He would have had to suffer repeatedly since the foundation of the world. But as it is, He has appeared once for all at the end of the age to put away sin by the sacrifice of Himself. So Christ, having been offered once to bear the sins of many, will appear a second time, not to deal with sin but to save those who are eagerly waiting for Him.

Something very interesting was recorded in the Talmud,[100] which may provide insight and credible evidence outside of scripture for the changing of the priesthood. The Talmud says that the rabbis taught that for the entire forty year ministry of Simeon the Righteous, each year the lot [for the Lord] always

---

[97] Matthew 27:51

[98] Hebrews 6:19

[99] Hebrews 7:19

[100] *Yoma* ,39b, *Babylonian Talmud,* Soncino Press Edition, from article by Ben Burton, *The Secret of the Scarlet Thread,* accessed at: http://ladderofjacob.com/2014/10/03/secret-of-the-scarlet-thread/

came up in the right hand, the crimson colored strap, or thread, always turned white, the menorah kept shining and the fire on the altar kept burning without adding wood. After Simeon's ministry (time of ministry not clear, about 200 B.C. or 300 B.C.[101]), the Talmud recorded that the lot [for the Lord] was sometimes in the right hand and sometimes in the left, the crimson colored strap sometimes stayed crimson and sometimes turned white, the menorah would sometimes shine and sometimes not, and the wood on the altar sometimes burned without adding more wood and sometimes did not.

So what is the significance of all this and why is it important? To get an understanding, it is necessary to have some knowledge of the duties of the priests in the Temple. It was their duty to make sure that the golden lampstand, i.e., the menorah, was to burn continually[102] and that the fire on the altar would also burn continually.[103] It was the duty of the High Priest to make atonement for the sins of the people every year on Yom Kippur (Day of Atonement), the holiest day in all of Judaism. He was to take from the people two male goats and cast lots for the goats, one for the LORD and one for the Azazel, or scapegoat.[104] I'm not exactly sure about the mechanics for casting lots, but if the lot fell in the right hand it would be considered positive for an accepted sacrifice. The goat on which the lot fell for the LORD was sacrificed for the sins of the people and the scapegoat would be set free in the wilderness after having all the sins of the people laid on it by the High Priest.[105] Another duty of the High Priest on the Day of Atonement was to fasten a thread (strap) of scarlet on the door of the Temple. The Talmud records that if it turned white, the people rejoiced because it indicated that their sins had been forgiven. The scriptural basis for this practice and belief was

---

[101] http://amazingbibletimeline.com/blog/simon-the-high-priest/ - Accessed August 18, 2015
[102] Leviticus 24:2-4
[103] Leviticus 6:12-13
[104] Leviticus 16:5-10; 15-16
[105] Leviticus 16:20-23

"...though your sins be as scarlet, they shall be as white as snow (Isaiah 1:18)."

Now back to the Talmud. It records that something very significant happened in 30 A.D. with regard to the sacrificial system in the Temple. For the forty years prior to the destruction of the temple in 70 A.D., the lot [for the Lord] always came up in the left hand, the crimson strap never turned white, both of which indicated that the sins of the people were not forgiven. Additionally, the menorah never stayed lit, the priests had to continually add wood to keep the fire on the altar burning; and, the monstrous doors of the temple would not stay closed, but would open of their own accord. These signs indicated that the earthly priesthood was no longer effective, thus obsolete, as scripture says.

The Talmud does not answer the question of what happened that was so significant forty years prior to the destruction of the temple. For a believer it is obvious, it was the death, burial and resurrection of Israel's Messiah!

Let me emphasize that the Talmud is not to be considered as equal to Scripture. All authority is in the Bible alone. It does contain valuable information and it is a powerful witness to the accuracy of biblical history recorded in the New Testament. For example, it notes that He [Yeshua] was "hanged on the eve of Passover."[106] However, the rabbinical teachings recorded in the Talmud erred greatly in its denial of His coming as the Messiah.

In Chapter Seven, we'll take a brief look at about fifteen hundred years of history of the relationship of Christians and Jews in the Roman Empire.

---

[106] Talmud Sanhedrin 38a

76

The roots of Christian worship go back to the very first Christian assembly with roots firmly planted in the Old Testament scriptures and Hebrew culture.

OLDEST CHRISTIAN SYMBOL

The oldest Christian symbol ever found depicts the menorah, the Star of David, and the fish. The fish interlinked with the Star of David and the menorah provides us with an important visual of how Christianity and the worship of God in accordance with the Way was linked to a sect within Judaism as expressed by the apostle Paul in Acts 24:14. This symbol was carved into artifacts, found in Jerusalem, which date back to the first century. The Greek word for fish is icthus which Christians in that time used as an acronym for Iesous, Christos, Theos, Huios, and Soter, which when translated means Jesus Christ, God's Son and Savior.[107] The fish is still an important Christian symbol today, which is found in many Christian publications, bumper stickers, etc., and reminds us of the words of Jesus, *"I will make you fishers of men* (Matthew 4:19)."

---

[107] Lamplighter, September/October 2007, *Anti-Semitism: Its Roots and Perseverance"*, Dr. David Reagan

CHAPTER SEVEN

PERSECUTION OF CHRISTIANS AND JEWS

Christians in America cannot begin to comprehend the work of God in the miracle of establishing His Church. They have little knowledge of the history of the Church and how much blood was shed by its founders. Many of them literally followed Jesus to the cross. Jewish and Gentile church fathers were martyred by various methods of torture and death, i.e., beheading, crucifixion, mutilation and being burned alive at the stake. Martyrdom was the fate of Peter in 64 A.D., Paul in 65 A.D., Ignatius in 115 A.D., Polycarp in 155 A.D., and Justin Martyr in 165 A.D., just to mention a few.[108]   All of the apostles with the exception of John were executed because of their faith. John spent years in exile before he returned to the church at Ephesus where he spent the remainder of his life. He died there about 99 A.D.[109]

Prior to the fire of Rome in 64 A.D., Jews were the major persecutors of the Church. After the fire, the state (Rome) blamed the Christians for the fire and became their primary persecutor. Christianity became a crime punishable by torture and death. Christians were considered to be atheists because they wouldn't worship the gods of the culture and, as such, they were easy targets. Although persecution is on the rise around the world today, Christians in contemporary America would find it hard to comprehend the depth of depravity and hatred that was pervasive in the culture of that time. It seems that the people in that culture were determined to protect their gods. (Note: gods that need protection?)   Christianity being

---

[108] *Persecution in the Early Church*, H. B. Workman, M.A., 1906, Chronological Table, Pg. 373
[109] *Ibid. Pg. 374*

introduced into this kind of environment was sure to meet resistance. In his book, <u>Persecution in the Early Church</u>, H. B. Workman said, "We have seen the persecution was no accident, but the necessary resultant of certain main principles in Christianity itself, which brought the new faith into conflict with the outer world." The result was that literally thousands of Christians were murdered in bloody and indescribable ways. Men, women and children suffered torture and death for their faith in this Jesus who had laid down His life for them.

Often death seemed to be the only respite for the believer. Roman law protected the remains of the dead as well as right of access to their tombs. Workman also said, "Just the law itself, by the safety it insured for the graves of the martyrs, assisted by the reverence of the church and the desire of the faithful to be buried side by side with the faithful dead, was the real force that dug out the catacombs."[110] Since these burial sites (the catacombs) were protected, they were often used by Christians as a safe place to meet and/or worship.

Of all the emperors who persecuted the Christians, Nero and Domitian were the most persistent and cruel. In spite of torture and persecution, the church somehow managed to continue and even grow. So much so, that Tertullian boasted, "The blood of the martyrs is indeed the seed of the Church. Dying we conquer. The moment we are crushed, that moment we go forth victorious."[111] Toward the middle of the third century, the power of Rome was diminishing and the Church was becoming stronger. Emperor Gallienus was anxious to put an end to the struggle with Christianity and was the first to issue an edict of leniency toward Christians in about 260 A.D. In the year 311, Emperor Galerius, on his death bed, being tormented by disease and guilt, issued the edict of toleration, which terminated the persecution of Christians. The gods that

---

[110] *Ibid. Pg. 259*
[111] *Ibid. Pg. 352*

he had defended were of no use in soothing his conscience. Constantine and Licinian were signatories of this edict.[112]

For the first three hundred years of Christianity, Jews were hating Christians, Christians were hating Jews and Romans hated them both. After his "conversion" (many believe it was a political conversion), Emperor Constantine put an end to the hostilities between Rome and the Church when he made Christianity the state religion. Steps were being taken to reform paganism by implementing Christian sacraments and institutions.[113] Priests among the pagans were making a mockery of Christianity. One can imagine that this was not to be an "instant" transformation.

These changes did not happen peacefully and war was the result. Constantine defeated Maxentius in October, 312, and his contemporary, Licinian, defeated Maximin Daza in April, 313 to turn the edict they had signed into an accomplished fact. In March of 313, Constantine issued the Edict of Milan, which read in part, "We have long seen that we have no business to refuse freedom of religion. The power of seeing to matters of belief must be left to the judgment and desire of each individual, according to the man's own free will."[114] Freedom was granted for Christians in Rome but not for Jews or for Christians who kept the Sabbath and the Feasts of the LORD. More about this in Chapter 10.

Christians were then protected by the state and Christianity would then grow even more rapidly which, in turn, brought on other problems. H. B. Workman said, "Then, as now, many Christians brought with them into their new religion the habits and faults of their old life."[115] It seems that it would have been impossible for pagan religion not to have an influence on the Church, which emerged from that time. Essentially, what

---

[112] *Ibid. Pg. 278*
[113] *Ibid. Pg. 280*
[114] *Ibid. Pg. 282*
[115] *Ibid. Pg. 167*

this amounted to was the merger of paganism and Christianity, which was enforced by the state. The results of this merger would lead to eliminating the biblical "holy days" as practiced by the apostles and substituting the holy days of the gods of Roman culture. The consequences thereof would only be revealed by history.

The Jews, however, in the centuries ahead would become even more persecuted. Church leaders, Justin, Origen, and Chrysostom seemed to forget that Christianity was rooted in a Jewish savior,[116] and that the disciples and the first church were totally Jewish. Early church father, Irenaeus, stated, "God has justly rejected them [the Jews] and has given to the Gentiles outside the vineyard the fruits of its cultivation".[117] I wonder which scripture reference he used to make this statement? There isn't one! Workman also said, "An intense hostility to everything Jewish is one of the marks of early Christian literature, most strongly emphasized perhaps in the orthodox writings, in the Epistle of Barnabas." When confronted on what to do with the Old Testament, "he [Barnabas] and his school boldly twisted it into a merely allegorical or spiritual narrative, which the Jews had misunderstood from the first."[118] Today many Bible scholars do not believe the writer of this epistle was the Barnabas of the Bible. I tend to agree with these scholars. It would be very unlikely that anyone who had spent as much time with Paul as Barnabas, would have such a twisted view of scripture. Regardless of the author, the teaching in this epistle was not in harmony with Paul's teaching concerning the Jews.

Church leader, Augustine, the 5th century Bishop of Hippo, was a "replacement" theologian, but defied many anti-Semitic teachings saying that Jewish believers in Yeshua should not be

---

[116] Holy War For the Promised Land, by David Dolan, Thomas Nelson Publishers, Pg. 23
[117] Dictionary of Early Christian Beliefs, 1998, David Burcott, Pg. 364
[118] Persecution in the Early Church, H. B. Workman, M.A., 1906, Chronological Table, Pg. 115-116

kept from practicing their Jewish customs. He challenged many anti-Semitic acts and teachings and "taught that Christians who harmed Jews would face the angry displeasure of God."[119] His teaching helped to curb persecution of the Jewish people until the time of the crusades.

In 1290 A.D. **(the 9th of Av),** the Jews were expelled from England and for three hundred years none were allowed in that country.[120] Jews were ordered from Paris and parts of France in 1306, the Rhineland in 1348, Hungary in 1349 and Portugal in 1497.[121] In Spain, forced conversion to Roman Catholicism was the norm for Jews who either converted or faced torture and death. The Alhambra Decree, issued March 31, 1492, evicted three hundred thousand Jews during what was known as the Spanish Inquisition, eviction deadline July 31, 1492, **(the 9th of Av).**[122] Three days later, on August 3, 1492, Columbus set sail for the west with his crew, which included a number of Jewish sailors. The land he would discover would become a relatively safe haven for the Jewish people.

There is evidence that Columbus himself may have been a Jew who "converted" to Christianity. Letters to his son, Diego, are still in existence today. On these letters, he wrote the Hebrew letters, Bet (ב) and Hay (ה) in the upper left hand corner. These letters were then and are today commonly used by Jews to say, "b'ezrat Ha Shem" (With the help of The Name).[123]

בה

"With the Help of The Name"

---

[119] Jewish Voice Today, September/October 2008, *Christian Anti-Semitism From Replacement to Reformation,* Pg. 19, by Raymond Gannon, PhD, Hebrew University
[120] Prophecy in the News, October, 2008, *After Centuries of Exile, They Came Home!* By J. R. Church
[121] Holy War for the Promised Land, by David Dolan, Thomas Nelson Publishers, Pg. 30
[122] The Alhambra Decree, issued March 31, 1492, Judaism 101 http://www.jewfaq.org/holidayd.htm#Note1 Accessed 10/17/2008
[123] Jewish Voice Today, July/August 2005

"Ha Shem" is used by the Jews in place of pronouncing the Name of God, YOD-HEH-VAV-HEH, יהוה– YHVH, or Yehovah, the Hebrew Tetragrammaton, which they consider too holy to pronounce. With the help of The Name/HaShem, the persecution and hatred of the Jewish people will soon come to an end!

God's timing for the discovery of America was not coincidental. Since its inception, America has been the safest place on earth for the Jews to live and practice their faith. Everything happens in God's time!

Over the centuries, the Jews in the Diaspora were often forced to leave their homes in order to survive. The classic 1971 movie, *Fiddler On The Roof* portrayed what it might have been like to be Jewish and have to abandon one's home simply to survive. The movie was based on the Broadway production of *Fiddler On The Roof*, which opened in 1964, and was the first theatrical performance to surpass three thousand performances in the history of musical theatre.

CHAPTER EIGHT

IN GOD'S TIME

Just prior to the crucifixion, Pilate told Jesus that he had the power to free him or crucify him. Jesus informed Pilate that he had no power except that which was given him from above. (John 19:10-11.) Jesus also said that the ruler of this world is coming and had no power over Him. *"I do as the Father has commanded Me (John 14:30-31)."* At the time of His betrayal, one of His disciples was going to defend Him with the sword when Jesus told him to put it away. Jesus pointed out that if He wanted, He could summon twelve legions of angels (120,000) to His defense. Then He said, *"But how then should the scriptures be fulfilled (Matthew 26:53-54)?"* According to plan, He was the Lamb of God, *"slain from the foundation of the world (Revelation 13:8 NKJV)."* GOD'S PLAN!!

Over the centuries the Gentile church has blamed the Jews for the death of Jesus, but perhaps they should recall how many times the church has sinned and is just as responsible for those nails that were driven through the hands and feet of Jesus. *"While we were yet sinners, Christ died for us (Romans 5:8)... "* That's you, me and all who acknowledge Him as Savior. So, why was there such persecution and hatred of the Jews by Christians over the centuries? How many Jews and Christians were killed from the era of Constantine and the early Roman Catholic Church through the time of the reformation for their failure to adhere to church doctrines, which were not the same as the teachings of the Disciples and the Apostle Paul in the first century church?

The Jewish people have been waiting for the same Messiah who has been revealed to us. They are still waiting! Doesn't it make sense for Christians to share their revelation of the

Gospel in patience and love with the Jewish people, and perhaps show some respect for those who have been given the responsibility for preserving the "oracles of God,"[124] a people God calls the *"apple of His eye?"*[125] According to God's plan this apple has eyes that can't see.

Paul emphasizes the Old Testament Scripture of Isaiah in Romans 11:8, *"As it is written, 'God gave them a spirit of stupor, **eyes that should not see**, and ears that should not hear...'"* Paul is referencing Isaiah 6:10... *"Make the heart of this people fat, and their ears heavy, and shut their eyes, lest they see with their eyes, and hear with their ears, and understand with their hearts, and turn and be healed."* Perhaps those eyes are beginning to be opened. As of 2013, there were 200 Messianic Synagogues in North America[126], 150 congregations in Israel[127] for a total of over 500 worldwide.[128]

Are we approaching the time in history when "the full number of Gentiles has come in,"[129] illustrated by the fact that many Jewish people are accepting Yeshua? In addition, Hebraic Roots fellowships and assemblies (Christians returning to the Hebraic foundation) are multiplying and growing rapidly. God is revealing His Word to Jew and Gentile!

One of the most intriguing questions and revealing scriptures in the Old Testament is found in Proverbs. *"Surely I am too stupid to be a man. I have not the understanding of a man. I have not learned wisdom, nor have I knowledge of the Holy One. Who has ascended to heaven and come down?*

---

[124] Romans 3:2
[125] Zechariah 2:8
[126] Chosen People Ministries, http://chosenpeople.com/main/index.php/jewish-roots/304-messianic-congregations-and-the-modern-messianic-movement
[127] Article by JewishIsrael.ning.com, http://jewishisrael.ning.com/page/statistics-1 [Charisma Magazine October 29, 2013Charisma Magazine October 29, 2013]
[128] Chosen People Ministries, http://chosenpeople.com/main/index.php/jewish-roots/304-messianic-congregations-and-the-modern-messianic-movement
[129] Romans 11:25

Who has gathered the wind in his fist? Who has wrapped up the waters in a garment? Who has established all the ends of the earth? **What is His name, and what is His son's name?** *Surely you know (Proverbs 30:2-4)!"* Perhaps we have reached the point in time when God is revealing the answers to these questions with added clarity, for both Jews and Gentiles.

Let's note that the first coming of Jesus was a <u>literal</u> fulfillment of God's prophetic word, recorded in the Bible and by Roman Historian, Flavius Josephus, in secular history as well. Doesn't it make sense that the second coming of Jesus and God's promises to Abraham, Isaac, Jacob and all Israel would also be fulfilled <u>literally</u>? Literal manifestation of His Holy word for the sake of His Holy Name! Regarding literal interpretation of Scripture, Luther, who is accepted by many as one of the great Protestant reformers, stated, "The Christian reader should make it his first task to seek out the literal sense, as they call it. For it alone is the whole substance of faith and Christian theology; it alone holds its ground in trouble and trial."[130]

In both the Old and New Testaments, God's prophets, Jesus, and his disciples, foretell of a day of judgment and the return of Jesus Christ. The same prophets who foretold the first coming of Jesus also foretold the second coming of Jesus. For example, the prophet Zechariah writes, *"Thus saith the LORD, I am returned unto Zion, and will dwell in the midst of Jerusalem: and Jerusalem shall be called a city of truth; and the mountain of the LORD of hosts, the holy mountain (Zechariah 8:3)."*

This is what Jesus said about Judea and Jerusalem in Luke 21:24, *"they will fall by the edge of the sword and be led captive among all nations; and Jerusalem will be trodden down by the Gentiles, until the times of the Gentiles are fulfilled."* Jesus prophesies a dispersion of the Jews which

---

[130] *Martin Luther and Scripture,* by Scott David Foutz, L.W. 9.24; Q in Wood, 164.

happened in 70 A.D. and, as prophesied, the city of Jerusalem was under the control of Gentile nations until the six-day war in 1967.

For almost two thousand years the Jewish people have been scattered among the nations while struggling to maintain their faith in the God of the Torah. In a real sense, the Jewish people have been refugees for almost two thousand years. Though persecuted almost everywhere they went, they were generally loyal citizens of the country where they were residing and contributed greatly to the culture. Yet their longing for their homeland never subsided. "Year after year around the Passover table, they would declare, 'Next year in Jerusalem.'"[131]

The late prophecy teacher, J. R. Church, documented several attempts by individuals to bring about the return of the Jewish people to their land. It was not until the nineteenth century that the notion of a homeland for the Jewish people began to take hold under the leadership of men like William E. Blackstone, D. L. Moody, Horatio Spafford,[132] John Nelson Darby, John Adams, Robert Browning, Benjamin Disraeli and William Heckler. William Blackstone is so highly thought of by the Jewish people that the state of Israel named a forest after him.[133] Heckler worked behind the scenes to assist Theodor Herzl who founded the first World Zionist Congress in Basel, Switzerland, in 1897. At this conference Herzl prophesied that the establishment of the Jewish nation would occur in fifty years. This happened exactly fifty years later when the U.N. voted on November 29, 1947, to partition the remainder of Palestine into two states, one Jewish and one Arab.[134]

---

[131] Prophecy in the News, October 2008, *"After Centuries of Exile, They Came Home!"* by J. R. Church
[132] Lamplighter, May/June 2008, *William Blackstone and American Christian Zionism*, by Dr. Thomas Ice, Pg. 9
[133] *Ibid.*
[134] Prophecy in the News, October 2008, *"After Centuries of Exile, They Came Home!"* by J. R. Church

Two thousand years ago, writers of the New Testament were convinced that they were living in the last days as was Martin Luther in the sixteenth century. Listen to the words of Luther. "I do not wish to force anyone to believe as I do; neither will I permit anyone to deny me that the last day is near at hand. ...For the history of the centuries that have passed since the birth of Christ nowhere reveals conditions like those of the present. ... There has never been such gluttonous and varied eating and drinking as now. Wearing apparel has reached its limit in costliness. Who has ever heard of such commerce as now encircles the earth? There have arisen all kinds of art and sculpture, embroidery and engraving, the like of which has not been seen during the whole Christian era. In addition, men are so delving into the mysteries of things that today a boy of 20 knows more than twenty doctors formerly knew."[135] However, had Luther taken into account the literal sense of all the Old Testament scriptures, he would have known that Israel would have to once again be a nation for the last day to be "near at hand."

So, why the error with regard to Christ's second coming in past generations? Every generation has faced its share of trials and tribulations and yet, God's timing for the last days had not arrived. Could it be the fig tree was still in a withered state? I'll explain that in a minute. For hundreds of years, prophecy teachers have been saying that time is short with regard to the second coming. One might certainly think there is room for scoffing but in every generation, God's message was the same. Don't be caught unaware! Let's note Peter's warning in his second letter that, to God, a thousand years is as a day and God is not slow about His promise but is waiting and not wishing that anyone perish. *"But do not ignore this one fact, beloved, that with the Lord one day is as a thousand years, and a*

---

[135] Excerpt from a sermon by Martin Luther, taken from his Church Postil, first published 1522, Reformation INK, http://homepage.mac.com/shanerosenthal/reformationink/mllk02c.htm, Accessed 12/22/2008

thousand years as one day. The Lord is not slow about His promise as some count slowness, but is forbearing toward you, not wishing that any should perish, but that all should reach repentance (2 Peter 3:8-9)."

An in-depth study of Bible Prophecy will reveal that just as God has fixed the timing of the sun, moon and stars, He has fixed Israel as His prophetic time clock. In Matthew 24:32, Jesus said to learn the lesson of the fig tree. When they become tender and put on new leaves, you know that summer is near. So, also, when you see the signs, i.e., false christs, false prophets, wars, famines, earthquakes, and the preaching of the Gospel of the Kingdom to the whole world, you will know the **season of his return** and the **close of the age** .[136] – Note that it's the close of the age, not the end of the world… *"As He sat on the Mount of Olives, the disciples came to Him privately, saying. 'Tell us, when will this be, and what will be the sign of your coming and of the close of the age* (Matthew 24:3)?"

In Mark 11:13-20, Jesus cursed the fig tree because it was not bearing fruit and it withered. In Jeremiah 24 and Hosea 9, the fruit of the fig tree is used to represent Judah and Israel. Although God had sent many messengers (the prophets) over the centuries, Judah was not yielding fruit according to God's plan, and within a generation of the crucifixion was punished and scattered throughout the nations. Do you suppose that on May 14, 1948, when the state of Israel became a sovereign Jewish nation again, that the fig tree became tender and started to put on new leaves? According to plan? Could that be why Jesus said to learn the lesson of the fig tree?? Could it be that God was beginning a restoration process for the whole house of Israel, i.e., Judah and the Northern Kingdom of Israel? Both nations had been scattered to the four corners of the earth!

---

[136] Matthew 24:3

Remember that in Chapter Five we pointed out that Paul referred to the *full number of Gentiles coming into the Kingdom* and *all Israel being saved* as a mystery.[137] Remember also, from the history review in Chapter Two, that Israel, aka, Ephraim, the Northern Kingdom, had been divorced, and was lost and scattered amongst the Gentiles. Jesus said, *"I was sent only to the lost sheep of the House of Israel* (Matthew 15:24)."* Ever wonder why He said that? He sent his disciples out and said, *"Go nowhere among the Gentiles, and enter no town of the Samaritans, but go rather to the lost sheep of the House of Israel* (Matthew 10:5-6)."* And yet, there was to be a harvest among the Gentiles... a harvest including Gentiles who would join themselves to Israel. Could this be the mystery Paul was referring to? *"For God so loved the world that He gave His only Son, that **whoever** believed in Him should not perish but have eternal life* (John 3:16)."* Could this "whoever" include the Northern Kingdom, referring to the lost sheep of the House of Israel, as well as Jews and Gentiles? God's word answers in the affirmative!

In Romans 16, Paul wrote, *"...according to my gospel and the preaching of Jesus Christ, according to the revelation of the mystery which was kept secret for long ages but is now disclosed and through the prophetic writings is made known to all nations, according to the command of the eternal God, to bring about the obedience of faith* (Romans 16:25-26)."* Note that Paul said the mystery was disclosed and made known through the prophetic writings. How is one to know the gospel, i.e., the good news, without considering prophecy? Now consider what Yeshua said concerning the sign of His coming and the close of the age.[138]

---

[137] Romans 11:25-27
[138] Matthew 24:3

Matthew 24:14

And this gospel [good news] *of the kingdom will be preached throughout the whole world, as a testimony to all nations; and then the end will come.*

The Gospel of the Kingdom will be preached... and then the end will come! From reading the New Testament scriptures we can ascertain that many Jews, especially the leadership, did not recognize the Messiah at his first coming... perhaps because they were looking for a king in the likes of David, i.e., a lion to destroy their enemies. In the place of a "lion" came a "lamb!" On the other hand, many Christians may not recognize Messiah at His second coming because they are expecting a "lamb," as depicted by the Church, when He will, in fact, not only come as the Lamb of God, but He will return as the Lion of the Tribe of Judah,[139] to smite the nations, and set up His Kingdom, as the "King of Kings,"[140] to rule and reign for a thousand years[141] from the city of Jerusalem![142]

In order for God's prophetic word to materialize, Israel would have to become a nation and that is exactly what has happened in His time and in our day. We'll look at this in the next chapter.

---

[139] Revelation 5:5
[140] Revelations 19:15-16
[141] Revelation 20:6
[142] Zechariah 2:11-12

Has America rejected the Lamb of God? Is this nation headed for judgment? I believe it's a very real possibility. God has always used a nation's enemy to punish that nation and America has been importing the enemy for many years now. Some are in powerful positions of leadership at the highest levels of this nation's government. The national media and many of our leaders are so politically correct that they will not even identify the enemy, which clearly is radical Islam.

Strict adherence to the Quran and Sharia law is not compatible with the freedom envisioned by this nation's founders, who sought to protect this freedom by law under the Constitution. The Constitution of the United States is being undermined and freedom hangs in the balance. Could this be God's coming judgment on America? Indeed, judgment is a possibility and judgment is not pretty. Every judgment in history has brought with it tremendous collateral damage. May God open the eyes of freedom loving people and, by so doing, change the course of our nation and avoid the promised wrath!

This nation is in deep trouble, so deep that it may not survive. Moral decay is rampant, i.e., fornication, homosexuality, pornography, etc. Though not the only sins at the root of this decay, these three tear at the very fabric that holds this or any nation together—the family.

In addition, this nation's debt is very likely beyond the point of manageability. Scripture says that the borrower is the slave of the lender.[143] Is slavery the destiny of the

---

[143] Proverbs 22:7

American people? The world is in the midst of great turmoil and I believe that if we are to stand on the truth of God's word, it is imperative that we know the truth and live accordingly, even if it is in conflict with our long held traditions.

CHAPTER NINE

MODERN ISRAEL: THE "BULLY" OF THE MIDDLE EAST??

If Israel had not been born as a nation on May 14, 1948, and the world news we hear daily was not so focused on Jerusalem and Israel, I wouldn't be as concerned or feel the sense of urgency for people to know what the Bible says about the time in which we now live. Immediately following His comments about the fig tree, Jesus said, *"Truly, I say to you, this generation will not pass away till all these things take place* (Matthew 24:34)."* The fact is ancient prophecies have prerecorded modern history. We are living in that generation!

Let's take a look at about thirty years of history leading up to May 14, 1948 and briefly go back in time to World War I, when Dr. Chaim Weizman, a Jewish professor of chemistry in England, developed a method of producing a synthetic form of acetone, which was very important for the manufacturing of explosives. Explosives are necessary to win wars! This chemical process would have been worth millions to the British government, but Dr. Weizman gave it to them offering to oversee its manufacturing. He asked only that the British government favor the reestablishment of his people in the land that, at the time, was referred to as Palestine.[144]

---

[144] Prophecy in the News, October, 2008, *"Coming Events Cast Their Shadows"* by Rev. P. W. Philpott, May 29, 1918

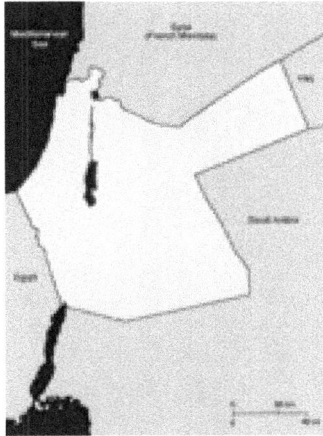

Israel – British Mandate

In 1917, British General Lord Allenby, a Christian, conquered the Holy Land, liberated Jerusalem, and set the initial stage for Israel's return to their homeland. Dr. Weizman's contribution of developing explosives for the allied war effort was a factor in the British issuing the Balfour Declaration in November, 1917, as proposed by the Earl of Balfour. The Balfour Declaration stated Great Britain's intention to create a homeland for the Jewish people in the territory of Palestine, which they had acquired as a result of a League of Nations mandate following the defeat of the Ottoman Empire in World War I. This proposal was endorsed by the League of Nations and United States President Woodrow Wilson.[145] This territory at that time included all of present day Israel and Jordan which is depicted in the map provided, captioned as "British Mandate." [146]

This proposal by the British and endorsement by the League of Nations and President Wilson was short lived. In

---

[145] Israel-A Nation is Born. 5 Part Video Series with Abba Eben (Israeli Ambassador to the U.N.), *A Personal Witness – Part I*
[146] "©Koret Communications. From *Israel's Story in Maps*, a project of Israel Insider (www.israelinsider.com). All rights reserved.

1922, the British gave more than two-thirds of that land to the Arabs which led to the creation of **a Palestinian state** called Transjordan which is known today as Jordan. [147]

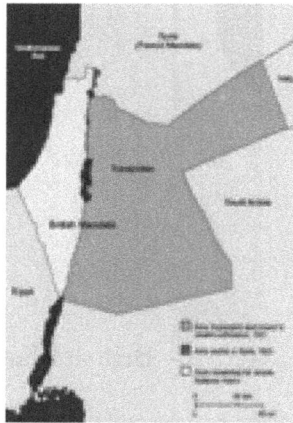

PALESTINIAN STATE OF TRANSJORDAN[148]

The Jewish people would linger for another twenty-five years, suffer through the holocaust in Europe, and wait for the world and the UN to mandate the authorization for a Jewish state in November 1947.

There were complex issues for establishing peace with the Arab people after World War I. The Allied Powers' defeat of the Central Powers in World War I led to the League of Nations Mandate, which divided the Islamic Ottoman Empire. The boundaries of the nations in the Middle East today are the result of this division and were influenced by the McMahon Agreement of 1915 and the secret Sykes-Picot Agreement of 1916.[149] The nations involved in this secret agreement were Britain, France and Russia. During, and after the war, it was their purpose to make sure that shipping routes remained open to supply their nation's economy with oil from this oil-rich

---

[147] *Lamplighter*, March/April 2008, Dr. David Reagan
[148] ©Koret Communications. From *Israel's Story in Maps*, a project of Israel Insider (www.israelinsider.com). All rights reserved.
[149] http://www.historylearningsite.co.uk/sykes_picot_agreement.htm

region of the world. The terms of these agreements were complex and the implications and effects are being felt and are being dealt with even today.

And now, after almost 100 years, the world is still preoccupied with access to Arab oil. The world is intoxicated with the black wine that's pumped from beneath the sands of Arab nations. The addiction associated with this intoxication is responsible for nations of the world jockeying for control of oil supplies, which often result in wars between nations because of greed and corruption associated with acquiring adequate supplies.

Subsequent to the horrors of the holocaust in World War II, the world's political machinery had to line up in such a way so as to allow the state of Israel to come into being. This was not at all a given. After World War II, British troops, in occupation of Palestine, were being attacked by both the Israelis and the Arabs in the Palestinian territory. For this reason, they were anxious to hand this problem over to the newly formed United Nations. The UN then set up a committee, the United Nations Special Committee on Palestine, UNSCOP, to come up with a solution.[150] This committee's solution was to further divide that land based on demographics and create another Palestinian state alongside or rather in the midst of Israel.

In my opinion, the UNSCOP "solution" was another attempt to appease Israel's Arab neighbors. This is simply not possible! It should be obvious to anyone who looks at the history of the Middle East that the current struggle for the land of Israel is not about the land but about an Islamic delusion of world domination and the subjugation and destruction of the Jewish people. (See map provided, "The UNSCOP Plan.")

---

[150] *Lamplighter*, March/April 2008, Dr. David Reagan

THE UNSCOP PLAN[151]

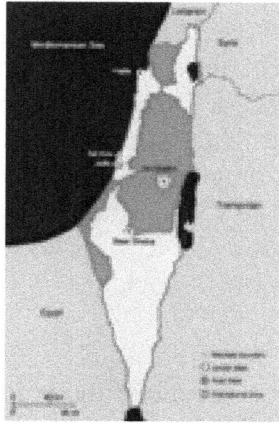

CAN YOU IMAGINE TRYING TO DEFEND A NATION WITH SUCH
BORDERS, WITH ENEMIES IN AND AROUND YOU?

No one knows why the Soviet Union supported this plan
other than perhaps they thought surely no nation could defend
borders as outlined in the UNSCOP plan. Historically, the
Soviet Union has not been a friend of Israel or the Jewish
people and perhaps they hoped the Arabs would annihilate
and/or drive the Israelis into the Mediterranean.

Today Russia is closely allied with Syria and Iran, who are
avowed enemies of Israel, and who have on many occasions
called for the annihilation of the Jewish state. A prophecy in
Ezekiel 38 and 39, referring to Gog of the land of Magog
(generally considered to be the land area of Russia), along with
Persia (Iran) and several other nations, says that these nations
will invade Israel in the latter days. *"You will come up against
my people Israel, like a cloud covering the land. In the latter
days I will bring you against my land, that the nations may*

---

[151] ©Koret Communications. From *Israel's Story in Maps*, a project of Israel Insider
(www.israelinsider.com). All rights reserved.

know me when through you, O Gog, I vindicate my holiness before their eyes (Ezekiel 38:16). "

In 1948, the U. S. State Department and all of President Truman's advisors, with the exception of two—David Niles and Clark Clifford---were against the UNSCOP plan. President Truman had been so troubled about the pressure he received concerning this issue, he wrote to one of his assistants, "I surely wish God Almighty would give the children of Israel an Isaiah, the Christians a St. Paul, and the sons of Ishmael a peep at the Golden Rule."[152] In March of 1948, Dr. Weizman, the Jewish leader who was by then respected worldwide, sought a meeting with the President to seek his support for a Jewish state. The President at first refused the meeting but changed his mind when a long-time personal friend, who was Jewish, intervened on behalf of Dr. Weizman. As a result of that meeting, the President assured Dr. Weizman of his support.

President Truman supported Israel against all political opposition and the United States was the very first nation to recognize its statehood on May 14, 1948, only minutes after Israel declared its independence. His support and decision to recognize Israel was not a very popular move in Democrat Party political circles and was of great significance seeing as how that year was a presidential election year.

The Democrat Party was split three ways in the 1948 elections. It seemed President Truman was almost certain to be defeated in his reelection bid. But "he who blesses Israel will be blessed."[153] Truman won the election! The Chicago Tribune made the mistake of printing its headline before all votes had been counted. Hence, a very famous picture of President Truman holding up a copy of the Chicago Tribune with the headline, "Dewey Defeats Truman."

---

[152] *Lamplighter*, March/April 2008, Dr. David Reagan -*Memoirs by Harry S. Truman: Years of Trial and Hope*, Vol. 2 (Garden City, NY, Doubleday & Co., 1956), P.157.
[153] Genesis 12:3

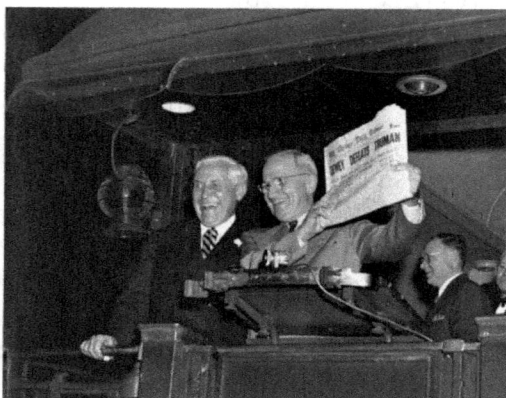

There had been great celebration in the Jewish communities around the world when the United Nations voted to adopt the UNSCOP plan by a vote of 33 to 13 on November 29, 1947. The UNSCOP plan was not to be implemented until the British Mandate expired in May, 1948. Although the Jews were not happy with the territory allotted them in this plan, they were willing to accept almost any plan that would give them a homeland in the land of their forefathers, Abraham, Isaac, and Jacob.

All of the Arab nations rejected the plan for plans of their own.[155] What the Arab nations didn't realize is that the God of the Bible has a plan that He laid out long ago. Many modern day miracles have taken place, which indicate that God is protecting Israel and its people. Israel's Declaration of Independence was proclaimed on May 14, 1948 by David Ben Gurion who was the executive head of the World Zionist Organization and Chairman of the Jewish Agency for Palestine. David Ben Gurion would later become the first prime minister of Israel. On that same day Israel was attacked by the combined armed forces of five Arab nations.

---

[154] Credit: Harry S. Truman Library & Museum. Accession Number: 64-861
[155] Lamplighter, March/April 2008, Dr. David Reagan

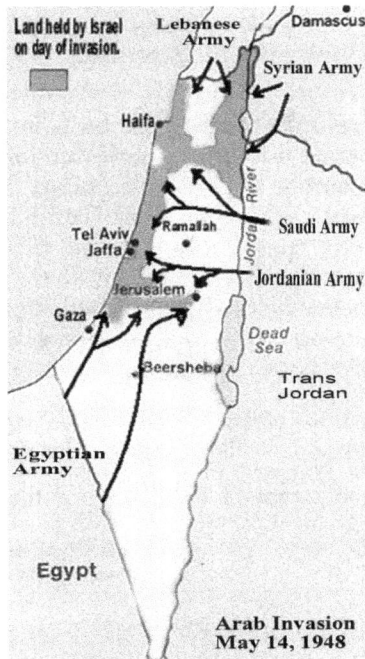

1948 ARAB INVASION [156]

Israel did not have an organized army and only a handful of smuggled weapons, but they miraculously managed to defeat the attacking Arab forces (35,000 strong) organized and equipped with British and French weaponry including armor and artillery[157].

The training and organization that the Israeli resistance forces did have was due largely to the efforts of British Officer, Lt. Col. John Henry Patterson and his leadership in World War II. He was considered to be too old to be a Commander in the British Army on the European front. At the urging of two

---

[156] University of Texas, Austin, Texas, public domain map, adapted by author to show 1948 Arab invasion; http://www. ib.utexas.edu/maps/historical/israel_hist_1973.jpg Accessed 12/21/2008

[157] Israel-A Nation is Born, 5 Part Video Series with Abba Eben (Israeli Ambassador to the U.N.), *A Personal Witness – Part I*

legendary Israelis, Ze'ev Jabotinsky and Joseph Trumpeldor who had served as officers under his command in World War I, he accepted the command of the Zionist Mule Corps for a second time. Though in his seventies, he trained and led into battle men who would become leaders, which included the first and second prime ministers of Israel, David Ben Gurion and Levi Eshkol.[158] This training would be utilized and put to the test in Israel's war for independence. More about Patterson a bit later.

Help for the Israeli ground forces would soon be on the way. Al Schwimmer, an American flight engineer for the U. S. Air Force Transport Command in World War II, smuggled thirty U. S. surplus planes to Israel in 1948 and recruited Jewish American pilots and crew members to help in the war effort.[159] This proved to be significant and helped to turn the tide in the war.

Even with the help of men like Al Schwimmer and John Henry Patterson, the odds for Israel's survival were far from certain. The world might look upon this victory as supernatural. Perhaps! But, with God, it's nothing more than performing and establishing his word.

Wars often result in people losing their property and possessions, and the Arab invasion of Israel in 1948 was not an exception. What is not known by most people in this country and other countries as well is that in addition to an estimated 670,000 Arab refugees who fled Israel in advance of the Arab invasion, there were an estimated 860,000 Jewish refugees expelled from Arab lands.[160] This information was reported in 2006 by Joseph Farah, of *WorldNet Daily*, in an article entitled,

---

[158] *Word From Jerusalem* newsletter, August 2008, *The Forgotten Refugees* by Casey Bar, International Christian Embassy Jerusalem (ICEJ)

[159] http://*UnitedWithIsrael.org/the-story-of-jewish-american-pilots-who-fought-for-Israel-in-1948/*

[160] *Word From Jerusalem* newsletter, August 2008, *The Forgotten Refugees* by Casey Bar, International Christian Embassy Jerusalem (ICEJ)

The Myth of Palestine.[161] Farah, who is an Arab-American Christian journalist, stated that most of the Arabs were not forced out of Israel, "but rather left at the urging of Arab leaders who had declared war on Israel." To corroborate his statement, he quotes the Jordanian daily newspaper, *Falastin*, February 19, 1949, "The Arab state which had encouraged the Palestinian Arabs to leave their homes temporarily in order to be out of the way of the Arab invasion armies, have failed to keep their promise to help these refugees."

Historical records show that the Jews actually encouraged their Arab neighbors to stay and live in peace. Even today, there is an Arab minority in Israel with representatives in the government of Israel. Many in the Arabic-speaking Bedouin and Druze communities of the Negev and Galilee serve in the Israeli Army and are considered by their Arab brothers to be traitors to the Palestinian cause.[162]

These original 670,000 Arab refugees mushroomed to over 4.4 million as of 2008.[163] According to the U.N. definition of "refugee," refugee status is not transferable to a refugee's descendants. On December 8, 1948, the United Nations established UNRWA, the United Nations Relief and Works Agency, which was established to deal exclusively with the Palestinian people This agency allows refugee status to be transferred from generation to generation **only for Palestinians**. Consequently, this refugee group continues to grow[164] and it is held hostage by its designated status at the UN and the Palestinian leadership allied with Israel's Islamic neighbors who want to eliminate the Jewish State.

[161] *The Myth of Palestine*, by Joseph Farah, Jewish Voice Today Magazine, March/April 2006, http://www.jewishvoice.org
[162] *The Sacrifice of Friends*, by Michael Hines, Word From Jerusalem newsletter, August 2008, http://www.icejusa.org
[163] *Word From Jerusalem* newsletter, August 2008, *The Forgotten Refugees* by Casey Bar, International Christian Embassy Jerusalem (ICEJ)

[164] *Word From Jerusalem* newsletter, August 2008, *The Forgotten Refugees* by Casey Bar, International Christian Embassy Jerusalem (ICEJ)

According to Israeli news source, *Israel Today,* Hamas was accused by the U.N. Board of Inquiry of using three U.N. schools run by UNRWA to store weapons and launch attacks in the 2014 Gaza War. U. N. General Secretary, Ban Ki-moon was quoted as saying, "The fact that they were used by those involved in fighting to store their weaponry and, in two cases, probably to fire from, is unacceptable." The article reports that 13,000 Palestinians are employed by the UNRWA and that 93% of 2,500 Palestinian teachers in UNRWA schools are Hamas members. The inquiry backed up Israeli charges that Hamas and the UNRWA in Gaza are allies.[165]

The largest contributor for funding the UNRWA is the United States and this funding is provided by the U.S. taxpayer. This agency's budget has gone from $540,000,000 in 2008[166] to 1.93 billion in 2012. Other major contributors are the European Commission, Sweden, the United Kingdom, Norway, Germany, and the Netherlands.[167] That is almost a four-fold increase—where is all this money going?

Farah explains, "They [the refugees] are merely pawns in the war to destroy Israel." He also points out, "There has never been a land known as Palestine governed by Palestinians. Palestinians are Arabs indistinguishable from Jordanians, Syrians, Lebanese, Iraqis, etc." According to a September 29, 1993, article in *The New York Times,* "In 1990, in justifying his support for Saddam Hussein's invasion and annexation of Kuwait, then P.L.O. chairman [Yasir Arafat] declared that the borders between all the nations of the Middle East are artificial and illegitimate, imposed on the Arabs by Western imperialists, and that there are properly no Iraqis, Kuwaitis, Saudis, Syrians

[165] U.N. Report Slams Hamas, by Aviel Schneider, *Israel Today,* August-September, 2015, Pg. 10
[166] The Official Website of the UNRWA - http://www.un.org/unrwa/finances/index.html - Accessed 9/14/2008
[167] The Official Website of the UNRWA -
http://www.unrwa.org/sites/default/files/All_donors_ranking_overall.pdf

or Palestinians, but only one Arab nation and one Arab people, whose common patrimony is all the territory of the Arab Middle East."[168] Isn't it interesting, this is the same stance taken by ISIS?

In spite of the billions of United States and United Nations dollars funneled to the Palestinian cause annually, the Palestinian Arabs are no better off today than they were in February 1949 following the Israeli victory over the combined Arab armies. Many international observers point out that the Palestinian leadership has, historically, used these funds for their own personal or political gain. Contrast the Arab refugee situation with the 860,000 Jewish refugees who were expelled from Arab lands and the additional 600,000 Jewish survivors of the holocaust who were all cared for by the very small and infant nation of Israel and integrated to become productive citizens of Israel.

Israel continues to be a beacon of hope for Jewish people who continue to suffer persecution in other nations of the world, such as, Russia, Ukraine, Ethiopia, and more recently in some places in Europe, etc. These people, upon arrival in Israel, are welcomed and taught the Hebrew language, given job training and integrated into Israeli society as quickly as possible. What about the seemingly abandoned Arab refugees? To quote Joseph Farah again, "There were some 100 million refugees around the world following World War II. The Palestinian-Arab group is the only one in the world not absorbed or integrated into their own people's land."[169] I personally feel sorry for these Arabs who are being used as political pawns. Why are they abandoned by their Arab brothers who are in control of so much wealth and land? If these refugees could only realize that they are not abandoned by the God of the Bible! His love would certainly include

---

[168] New York Times, Kenneth Levin, Newtonville, Mass., Sept. 29, 1993.
[169] *The Myth of Palestine*, by Joseph Farah, Jewish Voice Today Magazine, March/April 2006, http://www.jewishvoice.org

them, if they would only come to believe in Him and submit to His plan for them, for the world and for the Jewish people. But, it seems they are blinded by hatred.

Most of the world says much of Israel's land is occupied territory even though Israel gained control of that land in wars where they had been attacked by Arab armies who had rejected the UNSCOP plan in 1948 and in the defensive preemptive strike in the 1967 Six-Day War in which Egyptian and Syrian militaries were prepared to strike Israel and an attack was imminent.

It seems that Arab oil money buys substantial media influence and as a result the press is generally hostile to Israel. In general, Israel is depicted as "Goliath" and the Arabs are portrayed as "little David" with his slingshot. Look at the map provided. Just who is "Goliath??"

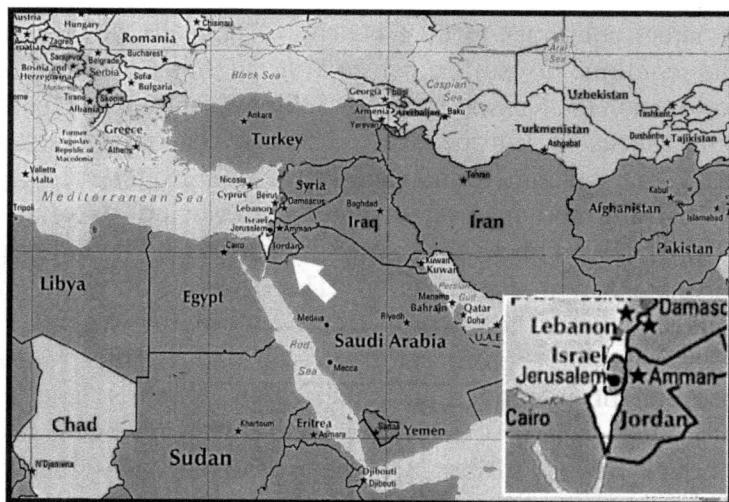

DARK SHADED LAND MASS SHOWS HOSTILE ISLAMIC NATIONS![170]

---

[170] University of Texas, Austin, Texas, public domain map, adapted by author to show Israel in comparison with Islamic nations; Accessed 12/21/2008

The land of modern Israel is shown as compared to that of the landmass of hostile Islamic nations.[171]   Can you find Israel?? (See the arrow and inset.) Arabs control 99.9% of the Middle East land. Israel represents 1/10 of 1 percent of the landmass.[172]   If it were not so serious, it would be laughable to think that the world has been duped into believing that the country represented in this tiny little sliver of land is the "bully" of the Middle East as portrayed in the news media. As you can see, Israel is surrounded by hostile Islamic nations. Egypt and Jordan have signed peace treaties with Israel; although a little shaky at times (particularly during the brief reign of the Islamic Brotherhood in Egypt), these treaties seem to be holding up. The rise of the Islamic State in Syria (ISIS) and Iraq is not only a threat to Israel but is also a threat to the governments of Egypt and Jordan. Real peace in this part of the world is as elusive as shifting sand!

The so-called Arab Spring, with the victory and then subsequent ouster of the Muslim Brotherhood in Egypt, the rebel victories in Tunisia and Libya, the ongoing war of rebels against the Government of Syria, the bloody brutality of ISIS in Syria and Iraq, all pose significant and increasing danger for Israel and its people. ISIS is in the process of committing genocide on the Christian and Kurdish communities in Syria and Iraq. The Christian communities there date back to biblical times. Regrettably, there does not seem to be any help on the horizon for these Christians.

Because of the obvious danger of being surrounded by hostile enemy forces, Israel reacts militarily only in self-defense which can include preemptive offensive force if necessary to ensure its survival. This could well be the case in

---

[171] *The Myth of Palestine*, by Joseph Farah, and *Why Not Divide Israel*, by Sarah Weiner, Jewish Voice Today Magazine, March/April 2006, http://www.jewishvoice.org
[172] *The Myth of Palestine*, by Joseph Farah, Jewish Voice Today Magazine, March/April 2006. http://www.jewishvoice.org

the future with regard to the current situation with Iran and its nuclear program. The current U. S. Administration and the U. S. State Department has approved a deal with Iran, without congressional approval, in regard to its nuclear program and this so-called deal is in no way beneficial to Israel. Can you imagine the courage it takes to live under the condition of being surrounded by enemies who have so often demonstrated their willingness to blow themselves up and launch missiles to indiscriminately kill and maim Israeli citizens? Can you imagine these enemies with a nuclear device and the danger it poses to the survival of the Jewish state?

Israel seems to be in a no-win situation with regard to public opinion throughout the world. When Israel responded militarily to thousands of rockets being fired indiscriminately by Hamas toward Israeli citizens in 2014, they were widely condemned by the mainstream media. The majority of the citizenry in Israel seems to be catching on to the anti-Israel bias in the media and are letting their views be known at the ballot box. Benjamin Netanyahu and the Likud Party won a resounding victory in the March 2015 elections, even though it was reported that substantial assistance was provided to his opposition by political operatives linked to the President of the United States.

Despite being overwhelmingly out-numbered in men and weapons, Israel continued to win wars against its Arab neighbors in 1956, 1967 and in 1973. Israel's victory in the Six Day War in 1967 was one of the most stunning victories in the annals of military history. For months leading up to the war, rhetoric from leaders in Egypt, Syria and Iraq were threatening the annihilation of Israel. Israel was surrounded by hostile forces and overwhelmingly outnumbered. On June 5, 1967, Israel launched a preemptive air attack destroying nearly the entire Egyptian and Jordanian air forces as well as half of the Syrian air force on the ground. As its name implies, the war was over in just six days. Israel's striking military victory

108

could be considered nothing less than miraculous. It came, however, at a very high cost. Israel had 777 dead and 2,586 wounded in just six days of fighting.[173] Proportionate to her total population, this was twice as many men as were lost by the U. S. in eight years of fighting in Vietnam.[174]

I remember listening to news reports about the Six Day War on the radio while I was stationed at Camp Casey, South Korea, in 1967. I even remember "pulling" for Israel back then. I don't know if it was because they were the underdog or if, without me knowing it, God had placed it in my heart that there was something special about this nation. At that time I didn't realize that the nation of Israel had been reborn and was less than twenty years old. I was only a child in 1948 and was not aware that important prophetic world events were taking place or of the biblical significance of the rebirth of the nation of Israel.

In the Yom Kippur War of 1973, Israel was in severe danger of being overrun in a surprise attack by the armies of Egypt and Syria. On October 9, U. S. Jewish leader, Max Fisher, urged President Richard Nixon to assist Israel. The same day Israeli Prime Minister Golda Meier placed an urgent call to President Nixon and stressed Israel's desperate need for arms. The President issued the order for and began the shipment of arms on October 10. His action turned the tide in that war almost immediately. On October 14, in one of the largest tank battles ever fought, Israel lost ten tanks in a battle that destroyed an estimated 250-300 Egyptian tanks. By the end of October a ceasefire was implemented.[175]

---

[173] The Jewish Virtual Library, *The 1967 Six-Day War*, by Mitchell Bard, http://www.jewishvirtuallibrary.org/jsource/History/67_War.html, Accessed 11/13/2008
[174] *Ibid.*
[175] Timeline of Yom Kippur War, by PETER EPHROSS, Jewish Telegraphic Agency, *http://www.jewishaz.com/jewishnews/980925/yom-sb.html*, Accessed 1/20/2009.

As a result of losing war after war, Israel's radical Islamic neighbors have changed their strategy to "terrorism," indiscriminately attacking civilian targets such as crowded markets, buses and restaurants. The terrorist armies of Hamas and Hezbollah supported by hostile nation states deliberately use civilian populations as human shields in order to gain international support in condemning Israel when Israel retaliates against their attacks. Suicide bombers have killed or injured hundreds of innocent Israelis, including women and children. Tourists from other nations have also been among the victims. In order to protect its citizens, and tourists as well, Israel was forced to erect security fences and check points to detect and stop the threat from suicide bombers. Israel has known little peace since 1948 and yet it continues to thrive.

Today, Israel is a formidable military power but because of international pressure, Israel is being coerced into trading land acquired in the 1967 war for peace. I might add that Israel has not had a decisive victory over its enemies since it began bargaining land for peace. This land was purchased with the blood of Israeli soldiers and is of strategic importance because losing it makes Israel's borders virtually indefensible. It doesn't make sense to give this land back to enemies who are hell-bent on your destruction.

In 2005, at the urging of President George W. Bush and the U. S. State Department, Israel's Ariel Sharon ceded Gaza to the Palestinians thereby uprooting thousands of Jewish families so that Israel could have peace with her neighbors. What has been the result of this Israeli pull-out? Syndicated columnist, Charles Krauthammer, has stated, "Look at Gaza today. No Israeli occupation, no settlements, not a single Jew left. The Palestinian response? Unremitting rocket fire killing and maiming Israeli civilians. The declared *casus belli* [cause of war] of the Palestinian government and Gaza behind these rockets? The very existence of the Jewish state."[176] This "land for peace" deal has resulted in two wars between the Israeli Defense Forces and Hamas in less than ten years in Israel's effort to protect its citizens in southern Israel. What a deal!

Only a day or so after the United States pressured Israel into ceding Gaza to the Palestinians, the U.S. experienced the most destructive storm in its history as Hurricane Katrina slammed into New Orleans and the Louisiana and Mississippi Gulf Coast. Could this be a consequence of the U.S. participation in this "land for peace" deal? As documented in the book, *Eye to Eye,* by White House Press Secretary, William Koenig, which I mentioned in Chapter 3, there certainly seems to be a very real possibility! Just as the Jewish people in Gaza lost their homes and were forced to evacuate, thousands of residents in Louisiana and Mississippi were forced to evacuate and many lost their homes to the massive hurricane.

Since the election of Barack Obama in 2008, his administration and the U.S. State Department, under Secretaries of State Hillary Clinton and John Kerry, have continued the policy of coercing Israel to give away land for peace. Tremendous pressure has been put on Israel to go back to their pre-1967 borders and cede the biblical heartland of Israel to the so-called "Palestinians," so-called because prior to 1967 the term did not exist. At that time, this land, which was referred to as the "West Bank" by the world media, was under the control of Jordan. Why is it that Jordan, an Arab state, did not establish a "Palestinian" state for their Islamic Arab brothers when this territory was under their control? Tragically, the answer to this question is that these people are pawns and, as stated by Mr. Farah,[177] are being used by Islamic

---

[176] Lamplighter, September/October 2008, *Observations About Israel Today,* Pg. 14, Published by Lamb & Lion Ministries
[177] *The Myth of Palestine,* by Joseph Farah, Jewish Voice Today Magazine, March/April 2006, http://www.jewishvoice.org

Arab nations to further their goal of destroying the nation of Israel.

Why do world leaders continue to think that they can make peace happen between the Jews and their militant Islamic neighbors? Over and over, these neighbors have demonstrated by words and actions that their goal is the destruction of Israel and the Jewish people. Israel has sought peace by making concessions that are too soon turned to the advantage of their enemies who continue to seek their elimination. Israel is a tiny nation, smaller than the state of New Jersey, and yet, as prophesied, Jerusalem is a burdensome stone for the world and Israel is the focus of the world's attention. *"On that day I will make Jerusalem a heavy stone for all the peoples; all who lift it shall grievously hurt themselves. And all the nations of the earth shall come together against it.* (Zechariah 12:3)*"*

Hardly a day goes by that one does not hear news that the UN is condemning Israel in one way or the other and calling for Israel to give up land for peace. Israel's Prime Minister, Benjamin Netanyahu, spoke to the UN General Assembly on September 23, 2011, and stated that Israel is more condemned in the United Nations than all the nations of the world combined. Still the UN continues to push for the division of the land of Israel. A warning from the God of Israel through the prophet Joel, *"For behold, in those days and at that time, when I restore the fortunes of Judah and Jerusalem, I will gather all the nations and bring them down to the valley of Jehosh'aphat, and I will **enter into judgment** with them there, on account of my people and my heritage, **because they** have scattered them among the nations, and have **divided up my land*** (Joel 3:1-2).*"*

In the first edition, I made the statement that most Americans do not feel threatened by Islam. This is no longer true. Americans are now taking notice of the demographic changes in the United States and Europe. Although many in the Islamic faith are peace-loving people, it seems that as Muslims gain superiority in demographics, many become increasingly intolerant and militant. The hard evidence for this in the United States is visible in the tragic events of 9/11, the November 2009, Ft. Hood massacre, the April 2013 Boston Marathon bombing, and the ISIS attack on a free speech event in Garland, TX, in May 2015. It seems that terrorist events are on the rise. In July 2015, four U. S. Marines and one U. S Navy sailor were killed in Chattanooga, TN, by an Islamic terrorist. This event prompted the Rev. Franklin Graham to say on his Facebook page, July 17, 2015, "We are under attack by Muslims at home and abroad. We should stop all immigration of Muslims to the U.S. until this threat with Islam has been settled." That's a common sense suggestion!

In some parts of the United States Islam is taught in public schools. Contrast this with the fact that teaching Christianity is not allowed in public schools in the United States. Consider also, there is zero tolerance for other religions in countries where Muslims under Sharia law are in absolute control. People of the Islamic faith resist assimilation into Western culture. They tend to set up their own communities where they ultimately seek to establish Sharia law, which then leads to areas of Muslim control like the "No-Go zones" located in France that have become more widely publicized since the Charlie Hebdo shootings.[178] Herein lies the danger for America and other countries where Islam has taken root.

The Koran, written in about 600 A.D., advocates submission to Allah or else... death or slavery! It teaches that Jesus was a prophet and that God has no son. The Bible says that Jesus is the Son of God and is God, in the Word, made flesh. How could anyone believe that the two are the same God? Any Christian who does is scripturally ignorant, or they dare to stand in opposition to God's word. *"Who is a liar but*

---

[178] *European 'No-Go' Zones: Fact or Fiction?* By Soeren Kern, Gatestone Institute
http://www.gatestoneinstitute.org/5128/france-no-go-zones

he who denies that Jesus is the Christ? This is the antichrist, He who denies the Father and the Son (1 John 2:22)."

European evangelist, David Hathaway, says, "The Koran teaches that the world must be taken for Islam by Jihad."[179] He references numerous chapters and verses of the Koran, i.e., Surah 2:187, 189, 190-194, 216-217; 4:91, 94-96… and many others. He says, "Islam divides the world into two parts – the House of Islam (those at peace with God--Moslems) and the House of War (non-Moslems – infidels)." Consequently, if you are not a Muslim, (Jew, Christian, Hindu, Buddhist or atheist, etc.) you could be a target of jihad by militant Islam.

The Old Testament of the Bible was written and recorded hundreds of years B.C. and details the struggles and enmity between the sons of Abraham (Isaac and Ishmael) and the sons of Isaac (Jacob and Esau.) The Arab nations are descendants of Ishmael and Esau and these struggles will continue until Messiah returns. Their struggles are not only earthly but in the spiritual realm as well and have been going on for thousands of years. The struggles have to do with the covenant promises of God and to whom those promises belong, whether to Isaac and Jacob or Ishmael and Esau. This conflict pits Allah, the god of Ishmael and Esau against the God of Israel. That's a subject for another book. Perhaps someone else has already written it!

By faith, Abraham became the father of many nations and by faith were his covenant promises handed down to Isaac and Jacob – Israel. By faith, the Jewish people in the Diaspora have longed to return to their covenant land but for centuries this did not seem possible. But, *"faith is the evidence of things not seen (Hebrews 11:1)."* As we will see in the next two chapters, this faith would be severely tested.

---

[179] Babylon in Europe by David Hathaway, 2006, New Wine Press, Pg. 51.

A little known fact about Israel's war for independence is that a number of Jewish American pilots volunteered for service. A band of brothers known as the Machal ("volunteers from abroad") helped to turn the tide in the war. This volunteer effort was organized by Al Schwimmer who is regarded by many as the father of the Israeli Air Force. The documentary, *Above and Beyond,* focusing on the heroic efforts of a group of these men who secretly joined this conflict at great personal risk, was recently released by filmmaker, Nancy Spielberg (sister of Steven Spielberg.) Schwimmer lost his American citizenship for violating the U. S. Neutrality Act. He remained in Israel and founded the Israel Aerospace Industry, and was pardoned by President Bill Clinton prior to leaving the White House in January 2001.[180]

At a special ceremony in December 2014, Israel's Prime Minister, Benjamin Netanyahu, honored British officer Lt. Col. John Henry Patterson, and referred to him as "the godfather of the Israeli Army." Patterson's grandson, Allen Patterson, led the effort to bring his remains from California to have them re-interred alongside his wife's, in a cemetery in Israel where many of the Jewish soldiers who served under his command were buried. He died in California in 1947 and his dying wish was to be buried alongside his Jewish troops in the land of Israel. He had served as leader of the Zionist Mule Corps in 1915 and in 1916

---

[180] http://*UnitedWithIsrael.org/the-story-of-jewish-american-pilots-who-fought-for-Israel-in-1948/*

took part in the campaign to drive the Ottoman Turks from Israel. This was the first organized Jewish military force in Israel since the Bar Kokhba Revolt in 132 A.D.[181]

Patterson, who was a Christian, had envisioned a Jewish army, which would be instrumental in fulfilling the vision of Zionist leader Theodor Herzl for a secure homeland for the Jews. He became personal friends with Benjamin Netanyahu's father who named his first son Yonaton (Hebrew for John) after him. Yonaton, or "Yoni" as his brother, Benjamin, called him, was an Israeli war hero, who died in the famous raid on Entebbe in 1976.[182] After flying some 2500 miles from Israel to Uganda, an Israeli commando unit freed 103 Israeli hostages on a French jet airliner, which had been hijacked by radicals associated with the Popular Front for the Liberation of Palestine. All seven of the radical militants were killed. Yoni and three hostages died in the operation.[183]

---

[181] *Word from Jerusalem*, International Christian Embassy Jerusalem, August 2015 Edition, Article: *We Salute You, John Henry Patterson* by Lucy Jennings
[182] *Ibid.*
[183] "Entebbe raid". *Encyclopædia Britannica. Encyclopædia Britannica Online.* Encyclopædia Britannica Inc., 2015. Web. 25 Aug. 2015
<http://www.britannica.com/event/Entebbe-raid>.

CHAPTER TEN

CHURCH DOCTRINE INSTITUTIONALIZES HATRED

The physical Israel which is today in the very center of the world's confrontations and divisions has not yet received that new heart and spirit that God has said He would give them. The physical "olive tree" has been replanted — not yet a fruitful tree, but the same could be said for the "Church" which is fragmented, divided, continues to doubt God's word, and hangs onto teaching which is not supported in Scripture. This teaching has undoubtedly led to centuries of anti-Semitism, which, in turn, has led to the deaths of millions of Jews and Gentiles, as well. Jews killed for no other reason than because they were Jewish. Gentiles were sometimes killed because their religious beliefs did not agree with Church doctrine and, at other times, were killed in collateral damage in connection with the extermination of the Jews. World War II and the Holocaust are a good example of this.

Throughout history, the consequence of acts of hatred for or toward the Jewish people has been destruction and chaos. The people of the world can't seem to grasp that the Messiah of Israel, born of the Tribe of Judah (Jewish), gave His life in the same manner as a sacrificial lamb led to slaughter, as stated in Acts 8:32 and Isaiah 53:7... not only for the Jews but for the whole world... *"For God so loved the world that He gave His only Son, that whoever believes in Him should not perish but have eternal life* (John 3:16)." In the 25th Chapter of the Gospel of Matthew, Jesus/Yeshua issued a warning... *"...as you did it to one of the least of these my brethren, you did it to me* (Matthew 25:40)." This scripture can refer to how we deal with our neighbors, however, the context here, as I'll cover at the end of Chapter 11, is the second coming of Yeshua/Jesus.

117

It seems that we could begin to connect a few dots here. He who touches Israel touches the apple of God's eye!

Why is there such a great divide between believers in the God of Abraham, Isaac and Jacob, i.e., Jews and Christians? Jewish believers in the God of Abraham don't accept Yeshua as the Messiah primarily because of the way He has been represented by Christianity. A true Messiah would never be one who changes God's Law, i.e., one who rejects the Sabbath and the Feasts of the LORD. To do so would disqualify Him as Messiah. The New Testament actually corroborates the fact that it was common practice for Yeshua and His followers to keep the Sabbath and the Feasts. Where did the Church get the idea to eliminate these practices?

Very early in church history, church fathers were claiming that the Jews were responsible for killing Jesus. The Edict of Constantine, 321 A.D., decreed, "On the Venerable Day of the Sun let the magistrates and people residing in the cities rest, and let all workshops be closed",[184] thus, the first statute with regard to the state's legal change of the Sabbath to Sunday. The 29th Canon of the Council of Laodicea, which convened in about 365 A.D., stated "Christians must not Judaize by resting on the Sabbath, but must work on that day rather honoring on the Lord's Day resting then as Christians. But if any shall be found Judaizing, let them be anathema from Christ."[185]

The Council of Nicaea was convened by Emperor Constantine in 325 A.D. Leaders of churches who followed the practices of the Church in the Book of Acts were not invited to the Council of Nicaea. This Council changed the celebration of the resurrection so that it would not be associated with the "Jewish" Feast of Passover,[186] a date God

---

[184] Jewish Voice Today, September/October 2008, *The Jews Killed Christ,* Pg. 4, Sarah Weiner, Editor
[185] Nicene and Post-Nicene Fathers, Vol. XIV, P. 148
[186] *Ibid.*

had ordained prior to Israel's exodus from Egypt.[187] We should know that **Jesus, the Lamb of God, was crucified at the very time that lambs were being slaughtered in preparation for the Passover**. (John 19:14-16) The date for recognizing the day that the Lamb of God had shed His blood as a covering (Passover) for the sin of all humanity was changed because it was "Jewish!"

It should be noted here that God refers to Passover as one of His "appointed feasts"… a "Feast of the LORD," not a "Jewish" feast.[188] These church doctrines became institutionalized and led to more hatred of the Jewish people. It should be evident that the historical facts presented in these last two paragraphs indicate that the fourth century church and Constantine made deliberate efforts to distance themselves from the biblical teachings of the first century church. A distance that would insure division among Christians (30,000– denominations), as well as between Jews and Christians, for seventeen hundred years!

Centuries later, Article 28:33 of the Augsburg Confessions, written in 1530, states, *"They* [the Roman Catholic Church] *refer to the Sabbath Day as having been changed into the Lord's Day, contrary to the Decalogue, as it seems. Neither is there any example whereof they make more than concerning the changing of the Sabbath Day. Great say they, is the power of the Church, since it has dispensed with one of the Ten Commandments."* We might note here that the Sabbath precedes the Ten Commandments and that this article specifically acknowledges that the "church" had changed the Sabbath. The day that had been set apart by God on the seventh day of creation (Genesis 2:3) was changed by the Roman Catholic Church!

---

[187] Exodus 12:18
[188] Leviticus 23:2

In Martin Luther's *Commentary on Genesis, he says* "God blessed the Sabbath and sanctified it to Himself. It is moreover to be remarked that God did this to no other creature. God did not sanctify to Himself the heaven nor the earth nor any other creature. But God did sanctify to Himself the seventh day... The Sabbath therefore has, from the beginning of the world, been set apart for the worship of God."[189] The question one might ask here is -- why, with this understanding of Scripture, did Luther not take a stand in support of keeping the Sabbath? Apparently, there was strong sentiment in the 16th century for keeping the Sabbath. This view was defended by Andreas Karlstadt, a contemporary of Luther and one of the leaders of the Reformation.[190] More on Karlstadt in Chapter 10.

At this point I would like to reiterate something I mentioned in the Foreword. It is not my intent to offend anyone of any particular faith or denomination. I have friends and family in practically every denomination and I sincerely love and respect all of them. My intent is to inspire a longing and love for Truth. For through the Word of Truth comes a knowledge of and a closer relationship with our Creator... *"Then you will know the truth and the truth will set you free* (John 8:32 NIV)."

The issue of keeping the seventh day Sabbath and the Feasts of the LORD has been an indefensible breach of scripture for the protestant, who claims "Solo scriptura" or "scripture alone." The Catholic Church does not hesitate to defend its authority for changing the Sabbath.

---

[189] Article, *Historians Speak About the Bible Sabbath and Sunday,* Commentary on Genesis, by Martin Luther, Ed. J.N. Lenker, Vol. 1, Comment on Gen. 203, pp. 138-139. Pathlights, P O Box 300, Altamont, TN 37301; http://www.pathlights.com/theselastdays/tracts/tract_22j.htm Accessed 12/29/2008

[190] Boston University School of Theology, Andreas Karlstadt,

http://sthweb.bu.edu/index.php?option=com_awiki&view=mediawiki&article=Andreas_Karlstadt&Itemid=360, Accessed 12/16/08

For example:[191]

Roman Catholic

"Which is the Sabbath day? Saturday is the Sabbath day. Why do we observe Sunday instead of Saturday? We observe Sunday instead of Saturday because the Catholic Church transferred the solemnity from Saturday to Sunday." –Rev. Peter Geiermann, C.S.S.R., *The Converts' Catechism of Catholic Doctrine*

"It is well to remind the Presbyterians, Baptists, Methodists, and all other Christians, that the bible does not support them anywhere in their observance of Sunday. Sunday is an institution of the Roman Catholic Church, and those who observe the day observe a commandment of the Catholic Church." --Priest Brady, in an address reported in the *Elizabeth, N J News,* March 18, 1903

"Sunday is a Catholic institution, and... can be defended only on Catholic principles... From beginning to end of scripture there is not a single passage that warrants the transfer of weekly public worship from the last day of the week to the first." –*Catholic Press,* August 25, 1900

"If Protestants would follow the bible, they would worship God on the Sabbath day. In keeping Sunday they are following a law of the Catholic Church."— Albert Smith, Chancellor of the Archdiocese of Baltimore, replying for the Cardinal, in a letter dated February 10, 1920.

---

[191] Sources: 119 Ministries, http://www.testeverything.net and Sabbath Truth, http://www.sabbathtruth.com/sabbath-history/denominational-statements-on-the-sabbath.aspx

There are many such sources that verify the 'perceived' authority that the Catholic Church claims to have for changing the Sabbath. The following are quotes from leaders of various Protestant denominations.[192]

Baptist

"There was and is a command to keep holy the Sabbath day, but that Sabbath day was not Sunday. It will, however, be readily said, and with some show of triumph, that the Sabbath was transferred from the seventh to the first day of the week, with all its duties, privileges and sanctions. Earnestly desiring information on this subject, which I have studied for many years, I ask, 'where can the record of such a transaction be found: not in the New Testament—absolutely not. There is no scriptural evidence of the change of the Sabbath institution from the seventh to the first day of the week." –Dr. E. T. Hiscox, *Baptist Manual.*

Church of Christ

"But we do not find any direct command from God, or instructions from the risen Christ, or admonition from the early apostles, that the first day is to be substituted for the seventh day... There is no command or warrant in the New Testament for observing it as a holy day."—*Bible Standard,* May 16, 1916, Auckland, New Zealand

Episcopal

"We have made the change from the seventh day to the first day, from Saturday to Sunday, on the authority of the one holy, Catholic, Apostolic Church of Christ."—Bishop Symour, *Why We Keep Sunday.*

---

[192] *Ibid.*

Methodist

"It is true that there is no positive command for infant baptism. Nor is there any for the keeping of the first day of the week. Many believe that Christ changed the Sabbath. But, from His own words, we see that He came for no such purpose. Those who believe that Jesus changed the Sabbath base it only on a supposition."—Amos Binney, *Theological Compendium*, Pg. 180 & 181.

Moody Bible Institute

"The Sabbath was binding in Eden, and it has been in force ever since. This fourth commandment begins with the words, '*Remember,*' showing that the Sabbath already existed when God wrote the law on the tables of stone at Sinai. How can men claim that this one commandment has been done away with when they will admit that the other nine are still binding?"—D. L. Moody, *Weighed and Wanting*, Pg. 47.

Presbyterian

"God instituted the Sabbath at the creation of man, setting apart the seventh day for the purpose, and imposed its observance as a universal and perpetual moral obligation upon the race."—*American Presbyterian Board of Publications, Tract #175.*

Southern Baptist

"The sacred name of the seventh day is Sabbath. This fact is too clear to require argument. Not once did the disciples apply the Sabbath law to the first day of the week, — that folly was left for a later age, nor did they pretend that the first day supplanted the seventh."—Joseph Hudson Taylor, *The Sabbatic Question*, pp 14-17, 41.

Perhaps it's time to get God's opinion, according to the prophet, Ezekiel.

Ezekiel 20:19
I am the LORD your God; walk in my statutes, and be careful to observe my ordinances,

Ezekiel 20:20
*and **hallow my Sabbaths that they may be a sign between me and you, that you may know that I the LORD am your God**.*

It seems that, by now, our vision should be 20/20 regarding the keeping of the biblical Sabbath. Did you catch this? The LORD says that the Sabbath is a sign between "me and you" that you may know that YHVH the LORD is your God. That's getting very personal. A sign, by the biblical definition, provides a visible mark or symbol of this relationship, much like the wedding band is a visible sign of the covenant relationship between a man and woman in marriage.

"So God blessed the seventh day and hallowed it, because on it God rested from all His works which He had done in creation (Genesis 2:3)."

God blessed the Sabbath on the seventh day of creation and set it apart. The prophet Isaiah records God's word and the importance of justice, righteousness, the coming of salvation, and the keeping of the Sabbath.

"Thus says the LORD: seek justice, and do righteousness, for soon my salvation [Yeshua, Hebrew word for salvation] will come and my deliverance be revealed. Blessed is the man who does this, and the son of man who holds it fast, who keeps the Sabbath, not profaning it, and keeps his hand from doing any evil (Isaiah 56:1-2)."

Isaiah continues and is including foreigners, i.e., Gentiles, in his admonition.

"Let not the foreigner who has joined himself to the LORD say, 'The LORD will surely separate me from His people;' and let not the eunuch say, 'Behold I am a dry tree.' (Isaiah 56:3)"

"And the foreigners who join themselves to the LORD, to minister to Him, to love the name of the LORD, and to be His servants, everyone who keeps the Sabbath, and does not profane it, and holds fast to my covenant—these I will bring to my holy mountain, and make them joyful in my house of prayer; their burnt offerings and their sacrifices will be accepted on my alters; for my house shall be called a house of prayer for all peoples. Thus says the LORD God, who gathers the outcasts of Israel, I will gather yet others to him besides those already gathered (Isaiah 56:6-8)."

Those who hold fast to His covenant will be joyful in His House of Prayer! As He is gathering the outcasts of Israel, God will gather others besides those already gathered, undoubtedly, referring to Gentiles. The Sabbath is an appointed time God set apart to acknowledge Him as Creator, and to worship and to rest in Him. God has established His Sabbath and Feast Days, i.e., Passover, Unleavened Bread, First Fruits, Pentecost, Trumpets, Atonement, and Tabernacles, as **appointed times**. These feast days, in Hebrew, are referred to as, Pesach (which includes Unleavened Bread and First Fruits), Shavuot, Yom Teruah, Yom Kippur, and Sukkot. *"And God said, 'Let there be lights in the firmament of the heavens to separate the day from the night; and let them be for signs and **for seasons** and for days and years (Genesis 1:14)."* The word seasons in this scripture is translated from the Hebrew word, *moedim*, plural for *moed*.

> Note: Strong's Hebrew word for *seasons*, 'moedim,' #4150, defined as: properly, an appointment, i.e. a fixed time or season; specifically, a festival; conventionally a year; by implication, an assembly (as convened for a definite purpose); technically the congregation; by extension, the place of meeting; also a signal (as appointed beforehand):--appointed (sign, time), (place of, solemn) assembly, congregation, (set, solemn) feast, (appointed, due) season, solemn(-ity), (set) time (appointed).

One might ask, why are these appointed times so important? To which the answer might be, to question God's timing would be to question His authority. It was of such importance that God divorced the northern kingdom of Israel.[193] Why? Because they had changed His appointed times and created their own feast days, which was the equivalent of idolatry.[194]

The prophet Amos tells us that God does nothing without revealing it to His servants, the prophets.[195] Scripture nowhere indicates that the Sabbath has changed. The Sabbath, the first of God's Feast Days, as listed in Leviticus 23, was not just for "Old Testament" times. In fact, the "New Testament" indicates that it was common practice to keep the Sabbath. *"As they went out, the people begged that these things might be told them **the next Sabbath**. And when the meeting of the synagogue broke up, many **Jews and devout converts to Judaism** followed Paul and Barnabas, who spoke to them and urged them to continue in the grace of God. **The next Sabbath almost the whole city gathered** together to hear the word of God* (Acts 13:42-44)."

"And he [Yeshua] *came to Nazareth, where he had been brought up; and, he went into the synagogue, **as his custom***

---

[193] Jeremiah 3:8
[194] I Kings 12:25-33, II Chronicles 11:13-14
[195] Amos 3:7

was, on the Sabbath day. And he stood up to read (Luke 4:16)."

As I stated earlier, the New Testament indicates that it was common practice for Yeshua and His Disciples to keep the Feasts of the LORD. Some examples are:

PASSOVER/PESACH
Matthew 26:17
Now on the first day of Unleavened Bread, the disciples came to Jesus saying, 'where will you have us prepare for you to eat the Passover?'

John 19:14, 16
Now it was the Day of Preparation of the Passover; it was about the sixth hour... then he handed him over to them to be crucified.

The Preparation Day of Passover was the day the lambs were slaughtered for the Passover meal. Yeshua was the Passover Lamb crucified on Preparation Day, the Lamb slain from the foundation of the world!

PENTECOST/SHAVUOT
Acts 2:1
When the Day of Pentecost had come, they [the apostles] *were all together in one place...*
Acts 20:16
For Paul had decided to sail past Ephesus, so that he might not have to spend time in Asia; for he was hastening to be at Jerusalem, if possible, on the day of Pentecost.

TABERNACLES/SUKKOT
John 7:2, 14, 37
The Jews' Feast of Tabernacles was at hand. ...About the middle of the feast Jesus went up into the temple and taught..

On the last day of the feast, the great day, Jesus stood up and proclaimed...

Passover, Pentecost and Tabernacles were pilgrimage feast days and all Israel was commanded to go to Jerusalem for these feasts; and, as these scriptures indicate, Jesus and His disciples did so. Are we not instructed to walk as He walked?

To look at the universe and the laws of nature, we see that everything is in perfect time and order. The sun, moon, and stars are all in perfect time and order. The law of gravity is precise. Violate this law and there is no grace period. I can personally attest to that! Fortunately, God is merciful with regard to His Torah. Just as there are consequences for violating the law of gravity, there are consequences for violating God's biblical laws. His will is that all of humanity would come to repentance, not wishing that any should perish.[196] He has given us His appointed times to acknowledge and worship Him, the one true and Holy Creator of all things in heaven and on earth.

In the next chapter we'll examine how church doctrine became institutionalized early on in church history. We will look at some of the effects and perhaps come to an understanding of the need for repentance.

---

[196] 2 Peter 3:8-9

CHAPTER ELEVEN

REFORMATION, HOLOCAUST AND REPENTANCE

I mentioned earlier the problems with which the church was confronted in becoming a legalized state religion under the Roman Emperor Constantine. I have not done an in-depth study of the history of the church for the 1200-year period between Constantine and the Reformation, but it is my understanding that during this time it was the church, assisted by the power of the state, that persecuted Christians and Jews and thousands were martyred. This period in church history was greatly influenced by pagan idolatry, moral corruption, ignorance, and self-indulgence. This is the church in which the leaders of the Reformation found themselves. For over a thousand years, the church powers in Rome kept the word of God from the masses. Any attempt to make the word of God available to the people was met with severe opposition from the powers in Rome.[197]

The Reformation was necessary and, very likely, inevitable. The first noted reformer was John Wycliffe who, in about 1382, completed an English translation of the scriptures, which was handwritten and widely circulated. Twenty-four years after he died a natural death, his Bibles were outlawed and as a result, his body was later exhumed and burned. Reformers to follow were John Hus (martyred 1415), Martin Luther, Dutch scholar Erasmus, William Tyndale (martyred 1536), Ulrich Zwingli and John Calvin.[198]

One influential reformer, who is often overlooked, was mentioned in the previous chapter. Andreas Karlstadt, educated at the Universities of Erfurt and Cologne, was an

---

[197] *How the Reformation Changed the Church*, by Dr. Peter Hammond, Frontline Fellowship, Capetown, South Africa
[198] *A Bible for the People*, The Plain Truth Magazine, April 1994

influential professor of theology and the Chancellor of Wittenberg University who awarded Luther his doctorate.[199] There must have been a certain friendship between the two because Luther's wife became the godmother of Karlstadt's son.[200] Some of Luther's theology was much the same as Karlstadt's. But Luther's seemed more conciliatory to traditions of the Catholic Church. Karlstadt wrote convincingly for observing the seventh day as the Sabbath Day according to Scripture. Luther referenced Karlstadt in his pamphlet, *Against the Celestial Prophets*, "Indeed, if Karlstadt were to write further about the Sabbath, Sunday would have to give way, and the Sabbath—that is to say, Saturday—must be kept holy."[201] Their theological differences on communion, infant baptism, and images in the church ultimately drove them apart. Karlstadt's number of published writings in Germany were second only to Luther's for the years 1518-1525.[202] The last seven years of his life were spent as a Professor of the Old Testament, rector of the university, and pastor of the University Church of St. Peter in Basel, Switzerland.[203] His writings substantially influenced Ulrich Zwingli, Thomas Muntzer and Felix Manz.

Muntzer was a founder of the Anabaptists. The Anabaptists were persecuted by both Catholics and Protestants

---

[199] Information Delight, *Information About Andreas Karlstadt*, http://www.informationdelight.info/encyclopedia/entry/TV/Andreas_Karlstadt ,Accessed 11/17/2008 and GAMEO, Hein, Gerhard and Calvin A. Pater. "Karlstadt, Andreas Rudolff-Bodenstein von (1486-1541)." *Global Anabaptist Mennonite Encyclopedia Online*. 1987. Retrieved 30 December 2008 <http://www.gameo.org/encyclopedia/contents/K3759.html>
[200] GAMEO, Hein, Gerhard and Calvin A. Pater. "Karlstadt, Andreas Rudolff-Bodenstein von (1486-1541)." *Global Anabaptist Mennonite Encyclopedia Online*. 1987. Retrieved 30 December 2008 <http://www.gameo.org/encyclopedia/contents/K3759.html>
[201] Article, *Historians Speak About the Bible Sabbath and Sunday*, quoted in *Life of Martin Luther in Pictures*, page 147, from Against the Celestial Prophets, by Martin Luther. Pathlights, P O Box 300, Altamont, TN 37301; http://www.pathlights.com/theselastdays/tracts/tract_22j.htm Accessed 12/29/2008
[202] Boston University School of Theology, Andreas Karlstadt, http://sthweb.bu.edu/index.php?option=com_awiki&view=mediawiki&article=Andreas_Karlstadt&Itemid=360, Accessed 12/16/08
[203] GAMEO, Hein, Gerhard and Calvin A. Pater. "Karlstadt, Andreas Rudolff-Bodenstein von (1486-1541)." *Global Anabaptist Mennonite Encyclopedia Online*. 1987. Retrieved 30 December 2008 <http://www.gameo.org/encyclopedia/contents/K3759.html>

for their belief in "believer's baptism" (baptism by immersion upon profession of faith). Ignorance and evil were demonstrated by some who considered themselves to be "Christian." Manz was executed by immersion (drowning) for his belief in believer's baptism, and was the first of thousands of Anabaptists to be martyred.[204]

Why the persecution and martyrdom of these Christian leaders? Stated simply, it was because they dared to defend the word of God and also to question and challenge the doctrine and teaching of men. One can only imagine a church without the word of God. Scriptural ignorance of the people and the priesthood could only lead to behavior that would bring out the worst in man: Inquisitions, expulsions, and crusades were atrocities that were carried out in the name of the church and by those who called themselves Christians. Although the crusades were meant to counter the onslaught of Islam, tragically many Jews were victims as well.

Luther, in his treatise, *"On the Councils and the Church"* said that the first mark of a true church is the possession of the word of God.[205] The Reformation with the availability of God's word brought with it light in a dark era and set the people free to serve the risen "Word". Nowhere in Scripture does it call for Christians to hate or despise their neighbors, be they Jew or Gentile. Should it be so hard to understand the Jewish aversion to Christianity when, for all intents and purposes, Christians actually drove them away with their persecution and hatred of all things considered to be Jewish? Looking back, this seems to be "legalism" in reverse. It's ironic that the first church, all Jewish, accepted Gentile converts **without requiring them to adopt all the Jewish traditions and religious customs**.

---

[204] Pocket History of the Church, by D. Jeffrey Bingham, InterVarsity Press, Pg. 124
[205] *Ibid.*, Pg. 122 and 124

Acts 15:13-21

After they finished speaking, James replied, 'Brethren, listen to me. Symeon has related how God first visited the Gentiles, to take out of them a people for His name. And with this the words of the prophets agree, ... ***Therefore my judgment is that we should not trouble those of the Gentiles*** *who turn to God, but should write to them to abstain from the pollution of idols and from unchastity, and from what is strangled and from blood. For from early generations Moses has had in every city those who preach him,* ***for he is read every Sabbath in the synagogues.***

James was suggesting a "grace period" for Gentiles and requiring only four fundamentals that were prerequisites of the faith. His inference was that they would come to know the Law over time as Moses was preached every Sabbath in the synagogue.

It's likely that the Jewish people did not respond to the Gospel because they would have been required to give up Sabbath worship, Passover and all the other "Feasts of the LORD," as they are referred to in Scripture. Jewish observance of God's appointed times was, in actuality, obedience to God's commandments. The Jewish people who practice their faith are fully aware that blessings and curses are the consequence of keeping or breaking God's Law (Torah).

Deuteronomy 28:1-3

And if you obey the voice of the LORD your God, being careful to do all His commandments which I command you this day, the LORD your God will set you high above all the nations of the earth. And all these blessings shall come upon you and overtake you, if you obey the voice of the LORD your God. Blessed shall you be...

Deuteronomy 28:15-16

But if you will not obey the voice of the LORD your God or be careful to do all His commandments and His statutes which I command you this day, then all these curses shall come upon you and overtake you. Cursed shall you be ...

Deuteronomy 30:19

I call heaven and earth to witness against you this day, that I have set before you life and death, blessing and curse; therefore choose life, that you and your descendents may live,

How could the Jews accept the "Messiah" portrayed by the Christian church over the centuries when that "Messiah" is portrayed as being opposed to the fundamental teachings of the Torah (Old Testament) – a messiah who condones and promotes the abolition of God's Feast Days and the changing of the Sabbath Day? For a Jew to do so would be a denial of the very word of God, which has been handed down for millennia. They were commanded by the Torah not to listen to any prophets, even if they performed signs or wonders, if those prophets led them to worship other gods.[206] The failure of the "Church" to recognize the *"power of the Gospel to the Jew first* (Romans 1:16)"* most likely led to its inclination to separate itself from everything thought to be "Jewish." To deny any part of God's Word leads to confusion, contradiction and consequential separation in the Body of Christ. So long as the Church elevates the doctrine of man over the Word of God, that will not change.

Three thousand Jews were saved and baptized into God's assembly on the Day of Pentecost that followed the resurrection.[207] These Jews had no problem in recognizing the Messiah as attested to by the Apostle Peter, in Acts Chapter 2. At some point in time, perhaps the Messiah, as presented by

---

[206] Deuteronomy 13:1-3
[207] Acts 2:41

the Church, took on an identity, which was not the same as the Messiah presented by Peter, Paul, and the apostles. Paul had warned the Corinthians about submitting to another gospel and that just as the serpent had deceived Eve by his cunning, they, too, could be led astray, *"For if someone comes and preaches another Jesus than the one we preached, or if you receive a different spirit from the one you received, or if you accept a different gospel from the one you accepted, you submit to it readily enough* (2 Corinthians 11:3-4). *"* The Church should heed Paul's warning, examine its teaching regarding the Messiah and be true to the Gospel and the way He is presented in Scripture.

Yeshua said, *"Before Abraham was, I AM (John 8:58)."* He identified himself to two of His disciples on the road to Emmaus using the "Old Testament" Scriptures. *"And beginning with Moses and all the prophets, He interpreted to them in all the scriptures the things concerning Himself* (Luke 24:27)." There was no New Testament when Yeshua was walking on this road; therefore, He was identifying Himself using the Old Testament scriptures, which are so often ignored by many churches today.

I believe that God wants us to be truth-seekers and that so long as we are honestly "seeking" the Truth, God will guide us and reveal to us what He wants us to know. In God's time, His word is revealed.

Martin Luther was an influential reformer in a church that was in much need of reform. He was also a scholar who translated the New Testament of the Bible from Greek to German.[208] Risking his life, he challenged the power of the church in Rome and stood to defend the word of God as it had been "revealed" to him. I emphasize the word "revealed." God's plan and purpose for Israel was not in line with Luther's timing. Later in his life, it appears that when the Jewish people

---

[208] *A Bible for the People*, The Plain Truth Magazine, April 1994

in Germany did not respond to his preaching of the Gospel, he became angry and recommended harsh punishment for them. When he published his treatise, *On Jews and Their Lies,* in 1543, he wrote that they [the Jews] should be run out of their homes, that their schools and synagogues should be burned, their Talmudic writings should be burned, rabbis should be forbidden to preach or teach under penalty of death, and that Jewish people should be confined to their own neighborhoods.[209] Words spoken in anger or disgust are not likely to have a positive outcome and these words would impact some of the darkest days in the history of the world.

History tells us that the Nazis used Luther's words some 400 years later to justify the holocaust.[210] (See Holocaust information.[211]) Sadly, the church (Protestant and Catholic) in Germany showed little opposition, and what opposition there was, was crushed by Hitler as he carried out his pogroms against the Jews. However, there were heroic Christians who resisted the Nazis. Oskar Schindler,[212] a Catholic and a member of the Nazi Party, used his wealth and position to save 1300 Jews. Corrie ten Boom,[213] a Dutch Christian holocaust survivor, helped many Jews escape the Nazis. Dietrich Bonhoeffer,[214] a German Lutheran pastor, became frustrated with the liberal theology of the established church in Germany and was a founding member of The Confessing Church. For his resistance to the Nazis, he was executed along with other resistors, Theodor Strünch, and Ludwig Gehre, and three high ranking officials who conspired against Hitler, Admiral Wilhelm Canaris, General Hans Oster and General Karl Sack

---

[209] Messianic Perspectives, Sep-Oct. 2006, issue, CJF Ministries, San Antonio, TX, *On Jews and their Lies,* translated by Martin H. Bertram, in "Luther's Works", (Philadelphia: Fortress Press 1971), Pg. 268-271.
[210] Lamplighter, September/October 2007, *Anti-Semitism: Its Roots and Perseverance",* Dr. David Reagan
[211] See Yad Vashem Museum website: http://www1.yadvashem.org Click on Auschwitz Album
[212] Jewish Virtual Library, Oskar Schindler, (1908-1974)
http://www.jewishvirtuallibrary.org/jsource/biography/schindler.html, Accessed 12/16/2008
[213] *Ibid.* – "Corrie ten Boom"
[214] *Ibid.* – "Dietrich Bonhoeffer"

on April 9, 1945. They were all executed only weeks prior to Nazi surrender in early May 1945.

Germany justifiably paid a very heavy price in their defeat in World War II caused in part by their cursing of the Jews. It should be pointed out that the events that happened during this "time" in history caused the Jewish people to cry out even more for their right to a homeland and perhaps shamed the world so much, that the world's political machinery lined up in such a way that it actually happened! This was one of the greatest miracles in all history. The fact that for the Jewish people, who were so often persecuted and then sifted through the nations to have their identity preserved for all these centuries was a miracle in itself. No other people or nation has ever been dispersed and scattered around the world for almost two thousand years and then **regathered to become a nation again**, and yet God's word said that this would happen! Just think about this for a minute! A people, persecuted and scattered around the world, yet maintains their religious and cultural identity for two thousand years. That's incredible! I believe this is attributable to God's purpose for Israel and the incredible love and cohesiveness of the Jewish family and the role that fathers play in blessing and teaching their children.

God revealed through the prophet, Isaiah, that He would accomplish His purpose. *"I am God, and there is none like me, declaring the end from the beginning and from ancient times things not yet done, saying, 'My council shall stand, and I will accomplish all my purpose,'*...(Isaiah 46:9-10)."* God allows man free will but also allows man to reap the consequences of his word, action and disobedience. Every incident of God's wrath recorded in the Bible is the result of sin and man choosing his own path and reaping the consequences. These same principles are true today. Israel had been warned prior to their establishment as a nation of the consequences of spurning God's laws. Consequences, as described in Deuteronomy 28:

Deuteronomy 28:58-61

If you are not careful to do all the words of this law which are written in this book, that you may fear this glorious and fearful name, The LORD [YHVH] *your God, then the LORD will bring on you and your offspring extraordinary afflictions, afflictions severe and lasting, and sicknesses grievous and lasting. And He will bring upon you again all the diseases of Egypt, which you were afraid of; and they shall cleave to you. Every sickness also, and every affliction which is not recorded in the book of this law, the LORD will bring upon you until you are destroyed.*

See also Deuteronomy 29, and Leviticus 26.

These are some pretty serious consequences! The United States Government and the Supreme Court has been and is increasingly in a state of rebellion against God's word, i.e., removing prayer and the Bible from schools, Roe v. Wade (which legalized abortions), and the recent ruling legalizing same-sex marriage. In this, much of the Church is complacent, or worse, complicit. Could the curses described in this scripture, and perhaps something even worse, be in store for the Church in general and society in the United States, as well? Without repentance, it is very probable.

For centuries, prior to the reformation, the church had been teaching that "the church had replaced Israel."[215] It is my opinion that far too many Protestant churches still hold to that teaching. Let's look at what God says about this through the prophet, Jeremiah.

Jeremiah 33:24-26

Have you not observed what these people are saying, 'The **Lord has rejected the two families which He chose'?** [Israel

---

[215] "Replacement Theology," also called "Supersessionism" (The belief that the Church has replaced Israel as the recipient of all God's promises and that He no longer has a plan for Israel, the nation or its people.)

and Judah] *Thus, they have despised my people so that they are no longer a nation in their sight. Thus, says the Lord, if I have not established my covenant with day and night and the ordinances of heaven and earth, then I will reject the descendants of Jacob and David my servant and will not choose one of his descendants to rule over **the seed of Abraham, Isaac and Jacob**. **For I will restore** their fortunes and **will have mercy** upon them.*

"The **seed** of Abraham, Isaac and Jacob" in this scripture refers to the physical offspring and not the "spiritual descendants" of Abraham, Isaac and Jacob. That is not to say that there are no spiritual descendants of Abraham, but here, the Hebrew word for "seed" is *"zera"* meaning posterity,[216] which means all succeeding generations.[217] In light of these words, how can the Church continue such teachings? It seems as though God has "all the bases covered" in His prophetic word. For every possible question a skeptic could have which might raise doubts about the truth of God's word and His plan for Israel, He has the answer in His word. It's prerecorded!

I believe that a church is required to repent just as individuals are required to repent when what they do is contrary to God's word. The word "repent" in Hebrew simply means to turn around and follow God's instructions, i.e., Law/Torah. By using the term "church" here, I am referring to the various denominational structures. Some churches are better at teaching God's word than others, although every church should be God's vessel shaped by His Word. As it is with repentance of sin in the individual, so it is with repentance of sin in the church.

When something is not true according to Scripture then it is a lie. A lie is sin! No one knows the full consequence of sin in

---

[216] Strong's Concordance, #2233
[217] Webster's New World Dictionary of the American Language, College Edition, ©1964, The World Publishing Company

the church because sin is like a cancer lurking beneath the surface. We don't always know where it will manifest itself but it does manifest itself in many ways. Lack of power, sickness, corruption, homosexuality, fornication, adultery, manipulation, pride, arrogance, deception, division, divorce, dysfunctional families, mistrust, hypocrisy, and selfishness are not endearing attributes that Christ looks for in His Body. Yet, such is the description of much of the contemporary Church. But there is a sure cure for every sin in the Body of Man and in the Body of the Church and that is, repentance—repentance that begins in the heart of every individual in every church. This body cannot be healed so long as there is sickness in its members. A real search and longing for His Truth which is not found in many traditions and doctrines of the church will bring about His forgiveness, favor, and blessings. Only God is able to bring about healing, but it will require humility and repentance.

If the early church fathers,[218] Martin Luther and others, who taught that God had forsaken Israel, could actually see Israel **regathered as a nation** as they are today, isn't it likely that they might repent and say, "Oh, Father, please forgive me for not trusting in your word!"? One could most certainly come to such a conclusion but then, again, we can look at the Church in the world today and we see much the same scenario. So much of the Church is still steeped in "replacement theology," and is still following these traditions of men. As stated earlier, Replacement Theology, sometimes referred to as Supercessionism, or the Doctrine of Spiritual Israel, is the teaching that God has replaced Israel with the Church and that all the covenant promises He made to Israel and the Jewish people now belong to the Church. As such, He has no present or future plans for Israel or the Jewish people. This teaching is wrong. It is not biblical and is a fundamental cause for anti-Semitism throughout the world.

---

[218] Ignatius of Antioch, Justin Martyr, Irenaeus, Tertullian, Origen. From *Lamplighter*, Sept.-Oct., 2007, Dr. David Reagan, Pg. 4.

Since Paul was appointed and ordained by Jesus to bring the Gospel to the Gentiles, **should not the Church follow Paul's teaching**, which agrees with Old Testament scriptures concerning Israel, instead of the teaching of the later church "fathers"?? Perhaps the Roman Catholic Church took a step in this direction as Vatican II (1962-65) and Popes since then have clearly stated, "...that God has not rejected the Jewish people, that the Jewish people are not an accursed people, guilty of deicide, and that they remain 'the people of the covenant.'"[219] This acknowledgement has not been accepted in many mainline Protestant denominations and is most often ignored. However, recently Pope Francis took a step backward with regard to Vatican II's statements on Israel as "the people of the covenant." He declared the Vatican's support for a Palestinian state, and on June 26, 2015, signed the first treaty between the Vatican and the "State of Palestine,"[220] which has not been declared a nation but will, presumably, have borders with land taken from the nation of Israel. This is in direct opposition to God's word and His promise to "the people of the covenant," and also a reversal of the Vatican II declaration.

Protestant denominations associated with the World Council of Churches have placed themselves in opposition to God's plan for Israel as well. They have involved themselves in a "movement" known as BDS, which translates to "Boycott-Divestment-Sanctions." The primary goal of this "movement," which is backed by the Arab League and the Palestine Authority,[221] is to promote a boycott of any company or business that sells Israeli products or does business with Israeli companies. Denominations associated with this movement include the ELCA (Evangelical Lutheran Church of America),

[219] Jewish Voice Today, September/October 2008, *Messianic Jews and the Historic Church*, by F.R. Peter Hoken, Pg. 9
[220] Israel National News article, *Vatican Signs Historic First Accord with 'Palestine'*-
http://www.israelnationalnews.com/News/News.aspx/197322#.VeSXFenpg20
[221] Hope For Israel Newsletter, Fall 2015, *A Movement to Boycott Israel*, Pg. 2

the United Methodist Church, the Episcopal Church, the United Church of Christ, and the Presbyterian Church (USA). This bias against Israel is a threat to its security and is influenced primarily by Palestinian "Christians" associated with the Evangelical Lutheran Church in Jordan and the Holy Land (ELCJHL). It is difficult to understand the "Christian" reasoning behind this bias because it is not scriptural. Who will these Christians turn to for help if, or when, ISIS comes to their neighborhood?

The vast majority of people who attend churches in this and other countries are simply not aware of what their church has taught historically with regard to replacement theology. This may be true for those occupying the pulpits in many of those churches as well. Most often the issue is simply not on the radar screen, so to speak, and the people are just not aware. Herein lies the question... What are the consequences of not knowing and agreeing with God's plan and purpose for His land and the people He calls "the apple of His eye?"[222] The evidence in Scripture clearly shows that God is patient and compassionate. But, it also shows that God is steadfast in purpose and that the consequence of not knowing and agreeing with His purpose for Israel, the people and the land, should be considered cause for great concern.

Would it make sense for a loving God who is faithful to perform His word and who is full of mercy and grace, to not show mercy and grace to the very people He had chosen to be a blessing to the nations?[223] How could anyone answer in the affirmative, in light of all the scriptures and promises pointed out throughout this book -- on which God would have to renege, in order for that to be true? If His word doesn't hold true for Israel, why should anyone think it would hold true for "Gentile believers?" Would it make sense for God to set such

---

[222] Zechariah 2:8
[223] Genesis 12:3 & 28:3-4

stringent standards for Israel in the keeping of the Law and then turn around and say it's OK for Christians to ignore it?

In Matthew 25, Jesus tells a parable of wise and unwise maidens maintaining oil in their lamps in preparation for the return of the bridegroom. He continues with another parable about servants who were each entrusted with a certain number of talents and how those talents were invested. These parables are laying the groundwork for the prophecy in the following passages:

Matthew 25:31-33
When the Son of Man comes in His Glory, and all the angels with Him, then He will sit on His glorious throne. **Before Him will be gathered all the nations**, *and He will separate them one from another as a shepherd separates the sheep from the goats, and He will place the sheep at His right hand, but the goats at the left.*

Then those who are at His right hand will be invited to inherit the kingdom that will be prepared for them. Jesus continues,

Matthew 25:35-36
For I was hungry and you gave me food, I was thirsty and you gave me drink, I was a stranger and you welcomed me, I was naked and you clothed me, I was sick and you visited me, I was in prison and you came to me.

The context here is the return of the Messiah... the Son of Man coming in His Glory with all the angels with Him and He is sitting on His glorious throne. When Jesus is asked by those at His right hand, when did we see you hungry and feed you, thirsty and give you drink, a stranger and welcome you or naked and clothe you, sick and in prison and visit you? The King, that is, the Son of Man, responds, *"Truly I say to you, as you did it to one of the least of these, my brethren, you did it to*

142

me. (Matthew 25:40)*"* Just who was Jesus speaking of when He said "these, my brethren?" Now, I am fully aware that everyone should apply these principles in dealing with their neighbors. By doing so, we are demonstrating God's love for the world. This is my understanding and opinion about this passage. Would God's love exclude the Jewish people? Picture this—Jesus was standing in front of an all-Jewish audience when He spoke these words. Again, the context of this prophecy is at the time of **His second coming** and before Him will be gathered **all the nations**! Could it be that He may judge the nations on the basis of how they treated His Jewish brethren? Could we make the connection here to the Old Testament prophet, Joel, where God said…

Joel 3:2
*…**I will gather all the nations** … and I will enter into judgment with them there, on account of **my people and my heritage Israel**…*

I think we can! Wake up, Church!! Churches, and by that I mean denominations as well as congregations, that put themselves in opposition to God's plan for Israel could very well find themselves in serious trouble. As an individual in one of these "churches," it's not a good idea to find yourself working against the purpose of God. And it may well be time to look for an exit!

✳✳✳✳

Another personal note...

In December, 1942, I was baptized as an infant in Trinity Lutheran Church, Twin Sisters, Texas, as were six brothers and two sisters. Trinity Lutheran Church moved north seven miles to Blanco in the early 1950's and I have been an active and an inactive member of this same church since baptism. Memories of Mom's sweet voice singing *Jesus Loves Me* still linger in my mind. Perhaps God used such memories to help get me off the wide road that prodigals travel. I've spent more years on "that road" than I care to recall. I would go to church on Sunday, sometimes, and hear the word preached, sometimes, and sometimes, it would even have a little effect on the way I lived my life. But most of the time? I would leave the word in the pew and in the church! That's not at all what God means when He says, ***"Hear"*** the word of the Lord. To hear, means to take in—to absorb—to live accordingly. In other words, to hear and do, and to walk as Jesus walked. If we do not, and I am speaking from experience gained while walking the prodigal's road, physical and spiritual scars are the consequence.

We traced my dad's roots back to the early 1700's in a Lutheran (Evangelische) church at Driedorf, Germany. My great, great grandfather, Johann Peter Triesch, apparently was a man of strong faith. He and his family immigrated to Texas in 1845. On his tombstone in the historical Old New Braunfels Cemetery is engraved, in the German language, the epitaph, "Goodbye for now, we are parted from this life on earth, May our Savior give us peace until we are together in eternity."

144

My family history on my mother's side of the family predates the reformation and includes a couple of Evangelische ministers. In 1897, my mother's parents, Henry Artzt and Augusta Bruemmer were married in St. Martin Lutheran Church, New Braunfels, Texas. Augusta's grandfather, my great, great grandfather, Heinrich Bruemmer, Sr., had helped to construct this church in 1851. It is the oldest Lutheran church in Texas and still remains as a testimony to the faith of early German settlers in Texas.

My great grandfather, fourteen generations removed, Ulrich Artzt, II, was the mayor of Augsburg, Germany, and in the year 1524, authorized the first Lutheran preacher, Pastor Urbanus Rhegius, to hold a meeting and preach the Lutheran doctrine in Augsburg.

According to family history, Ulrich Artzt II was re-elected to a two-year term, which began in 1528 and would almost certainly have been involved in planning for the Diet of Augsburg, which drafted the famous Augsburg Confession in 1530. This document is the foundational doctrine of Lutheran faith and belief.

I point out all of this only to show that my "Lutheran" roots run pretty deep. Not all, but most people, are born into whatever happens to be the faith of their parents. I am truly grateful for my parents bringing me up with the fear of God. There is no telling where I might be if not for their perseverance in teaching me the love of Jesus and the scriptural foundation of right and wrong. They taught my brothers, sisters, and myself, according to the traditions of the Lutheran Church which they had inherited from their parents. Most teachings were fundamental to Christianity, i.e., honesty, integrity, and to love your neighbor, etc., however, they never questioned the origin of certain traditions, and neither did I for most of my life.

While attending Confirmation Classes as a teenager, I remember wondering about and maybe even asking the question, "Why are we not keeping the Sabbath?" I don't remember what the answer was or even if I received one. So, I continued to faithfully (sometimes) go to church on Sunday because that was what my family had always done. That was the tradition that had been handed down for centuries in my family. Over thirty-five years ago I considered and learned a little about keeping the Sabbath but I never followed through. Incidentally, my wife had followed the same path quite some time before we met. Around the year 2000, I began to seriously study the Bible, both the Old and New Testaments and found that God's Word is one from beginning to end. One supports the other, and God does not change! That eventually led to my understanding of the importance of keeping God's Sabbath, His Feasts, and in following His dietary instructions. It's really not that hard. But it is sometimes difficult to explain to family and friends.

CHAPTER TWELVE

AGAINST THE PURPOSE OF GOD

Wouldn't it be great if we had the ability to see and act through our hindsight and the foresight to do so? If we could see history in our headlights instead of our rearview mirror, then perhaps events like inquisitions and holocausts would not happen. Could you imagine the blessing God would pour out on the Church and the world **IF ALL TRUTH in God's word were at the very core of its belief and teaching**?? How many of those who are outside the Church might be attracted by and called into that "Spirit of Truth?" If believers could come to the understanding that Paul expressed in Romans, then perhaps we would be a step closer to that Spirit of Truth. *"Now if their trespass means riches for the world, and if their failure means riches for the Gentiles, how much more will their full inclusion mean* (Romans 11:12)?" According to Paul, "full inclusion" would mean greater riches for the world.

Shouldn't every believer be praying for the Jewish people to recognize Yeshua as the Son of God, i.e., "full inclusion," rather than blaming them for the death of the Messiah? As I have already stated, no one had the power to take the life of the Messiah. As the Scripture clearly says, He laid down His life as the sacrificial Lamb of God. The Jews, as well as the Romans, were instruments used to accomplish God's purpose to save the world: *"For God so loved the world that He gave His only Son, that whoever believes in Him should not perish but have eternal life (John 3:16)."*

In his *Preface to Romans*, Martin Luther said this about Paul's teaching in Romans, Chapter 11,[224] "But God is steadfast; his providence will not fail, and **no one can prevent its realization**." He also said, "There is a proper measure, **time, and age** for understanding every doctrine." (Emphasis mine.) It's hard to understand why, while Luther had this understanding of God's sovereignty and timing, he would clearly align himself in opposition to Paul's teaching about Israel.

It may seem to the reader that I am defending and holding up the Jewish people and Judaism over Christians and Christianity. Be assured that is not the case. My point is simply that we should focus on the log in our own eye before trying to remove the speck in the eyes of the Jews. To the Christians, that speck may seem big, but it's not up to us to remove it. That is God's responsibility. The Jewish people have many of the same problems today that they had when Yeshua upbraided the Pharisees for holding to the traditions of men rather than to the Word of God.[225] Christianity does the same. It is my understanding that many rabbis hold to the teaching of the oral Law, the Talmud, as greater than that of the Tanakh (Old Testament scriptures.) I do not agree with that. It is certainly possible that there could be valuable lessons and good information in some of these centuries-old rabbinic writings, but these should not be considered to be equal to the Scriptures themselves. Deuteronomy 4:2 cautions us, *"Do not add to what I command you and do not subtract from it, but keep the commands of the Lord your God that I give you."* To put the teachings of Man above the Word of God is a dangerous thing indeed.

Today, Christians who believe that God has not changed His mind about Israel and that the Jewish people have a right to

---

[224] http://www.ccel.org/l/luther/romans/pref_romans.html, Translated by Bro. Andrew Thornton, OSB, accessed 11/11/2008
[225] Matthew 15:1; 6,7

the land that God has given them are castigated in the news media and also by other Christians. Those who believe that the prophecies in the Bible are true, specifically that God has given the Holy Land of Israel to the Jewish people and they have a God-given right to live there, are often referred to derogatorily as "Zionists." So, why the negativity about Zion? Those who use this kind of negativity could very well be aligning themselves **against the purpose of God**. God, Himself, has chosen Zion!!

Psalm 132:13-14
For the LORD has chosen Zion; He has desired it for His habitation: 'This is my resting place forever; here I will dwell...'

Psalm 87:1-2
On the holy mount stands the city He founded; the Lord loves the gates of Zion more than all the dwelling places of Jacob.

Zechariah 2:11-12
*And many nations shall join themselves to the LORD in that day and shall be My people; and I will dwell in the midst of you, and you shall know that the LORD of Hosts has sent Me to you. And the LORD will inherit Judah as His portion in the holy land, and **will again** choose Jerusalem.*

Why is it that people who search the Scriptures and take God's word on this topic seriously are so often belittled and looked down upon by other Christians? Could it be a lack of knowledge? Or, perhaps those Christians hold the doctrine and teaching of man as greater than the word of God. It seems to me that when the time comes to face our Creator God, it would be a frightening prospect to have upheld and/or taught a doctrine that is against His plan and purpose.

"Remember this and consider, recall it to mind you transgressors, remember the former things of old; for I am God, and there is no other; I am God, and there is none like me, declaring the end from the beginning and from ancient times things not yet done, saying 'my counsel shall stand, and I will accomplish all my purpose, '... (Isaiah 46:8-10)"

Isaiah seems to be calling those who align themselves against God's purpose "transgressors" referring perhaps to those who hold to traditions of men rather than holding to God's counsel, i.e., instructions. God says through the prophet Jeremiah,

"O LORD my strength and my stronghold, my refuge in the day of trouble, to thee shall the nations come from the ends of the earth and say: **_'Our fathers have inherited nothing but lies_**_, worthless things in which there is no profit. Can man make for himself gods? Such are no gods!' Therefore behold, I will make them know, this once I will make them know my power and my might, and they shall know that my name is the LORD (Jeremiah 16:19-21). "*

Did you catch that? The nations shall say our fathers have inherited nothing but lies. That word 'nations' here is translated from the Hebrew word, 'goy,' the plural form is 'goyim,' which also means Gentiles. The King James Version translates this word as "Gentiles." What lies could Jeremiah be talking about? What is the church not doing today that was done by the church in the Book of Acts? Could it be that the church has been handing down and following the traditions of men established by some of the early church fathers, Constantine, and the Catholic Church, rather than keeping God's Sabbath, His Feast Days, and His dietary instructions?

150

The question one might ask is, will the church come to realize the need for change? As pointed out previously, God says He will "accomplish His purpose."

> "Here is a call for the endurance of the saints, those who keep the commandments of God and the faith of Jesus (Revelation 14:12)."

As the world continues amidst wars, struggles and confusion, most people are not aware that the nations are aligning themselves exactly as described in prophetic scriptures for "the last days." There are many prophetic Bible scholars who are in agreement that we are in "that Day" and, that "these are the days of Elijah" as referenced in the Bible and in the popular Christian song. Speaking of the last days, listen to God's last words in the Old Testament.

> "**Remember the Law of Moses**, my servant, which I commanded him in Horeb for all Israel, with the statutes and judgments. Behold, I will send you Elijah the prophet before the coming of the great and dreadful day of the Lord. And he will turn the hearts of the fathers to the children and the hearts of the children to their fathers. Lest I come and strike the earth with a curse (Malachi 4:4-6 NKJV)."

Isn't it interesting that the very last words that God gave to us in the "Old" Testament –BEFORE He gave us a "New" Testament—is… "remember the Law of my servant, Moses." We would do well to do just that—to actually be a part of the restoration of all things.

Elijah is to prepare the way for Yeshua to come again—to prepare the hearts of the people to seek the Truth—to seek Yeshua, to follow and worship Him in spirit and in truth, just as His disciples and the people of "the Way" did in the first century Church. *"God is spirit and those who worship Him must worship in Spirit and truth (John 4:24)."*

The Reformation, of which Martin Luther was a leader, was much needed, but fell far short of the *restoration of all things* as prophesied in Malachi 4:5 and Matthew 17:11.

> *"Jesus answered and said to them, 'Indeed Elijah is coming first and will restore all things...'* (Matthew 17:11 NKJV)."

Psalm 111:10
*The fear of the LORD is **the beginning of wisdom**; a good understanding have all those who practice it. His praise endures forever!*

CHAPTER THIRTEEN

WHERE IS THE WISE MAN?

Believers are called to witness to the truth of God's word from Genesis to Revelation. From the Book of John, we know that in the beginning was the Word, and the Word (Jesus) became flesh and dwelt among us. (John 1:1 & 1:14) It's hard for many people to comprehend that before Moses recorded the Torah (the Law, the first five books in the Old Testament). Yeshua/Jesus was there. Not only was He there, but He spoke the actual words which were recorded. Jesus told us in John 8:58 that *"before Abraham was I AM."* We are told in both the Old and New Testaments that God does not change. (Malachi 3:6 and Hebrews 13:8.) If He were to change, then He would be less than a God who could be depended upon to be our Rock. Yeshua, our Rock, said that He is the Aleph (**א**) and the Tav (**ת**), the beginning and the end. In other words, He was there before time and He'll be there for all time. He is not limited by the boundaries of time, and this would explain how He could tell us "the end from the beginning?" **את**

Perhaps here we need the insight and faith of Job who said to God, *"I know that you can do all things; no plan of yours can be thwarted* (Job 42:2 NIV)." Or maybe we'll get to the point where we can say as he said, *"My ears had heard of you but now my eyes have seen you* (Job 42:5 NIV)…"

In the garden, Adam and Eve were not to partake of the *"tree of the knowledge of good and evil* (Genesis 2:17)." God has not entrusted us with knowledge of all things. If this were not the case, we might think we could walk by knowledge and not by faith to obtain salvation, which is eternal life in the presence of God. Having this knowledge without having the

153

heart of God would most assuredly lead to chaos and all sorts of evil. To prevent this, God gives us His heart, the gift of a spiritual heart, when we are born anew by faith **believing in His Son** who voluntarily went to the cross and gave Himself for all.

> *"Jesus answered him, 'Truly, truly, I say to you, unless one is born anew, you cannot see the Kingdom of God' (John 3:3)."*

> *"For God so loved the world that He gave His only Son, that whoever believes in Him should not perish but have eternal life (John 3:16)."*

To acknowledge and accept His gift is the ONLY way to get anywhere near the Father. *"I am the way, the truth, and the life. No one comes to the Father except through Me (John 14:6 NKJV)."*

Like Paul, we should give glory to God. *"O the depth of the riches and wisdom and knowledge of God! How unsearchable are His judgments and how inscrutable are His ways. 'For who has known the mind of the Lord, or who has been His counselor?' 'Or who has given a gift to Him that He might be repaid?' For from Him and through Him and to Him are all things. To Him be glory forever. Amen (Romans 11:33-36)."*

How inscrutable are God's ways? How much higher are His thoughts than ours?[226] He even makes provision for the sin of ignorance, i.e., sinning when we don't know we're sinning… whether it be a congregation or an individual.

---

[226] Isaiah 55:9

154

Numbers 15:22, 24, 25, 26, 27

22 But if you err, and do not observe all these commandments... 24 then if it was done unwittingly... 25 the priest shall make atonement... and they shall be forgiven; because it was an error... 26 and all the congregation of the people of Israel shall be forgiven, and the stranger who sojourns among them... 27 if one person sins unwittingly 28 the priest shall make atonement; and he shall be forgiven.

Read this scripture in context: Numbers 15:22-31

As we learned from our study of Hebrews in Chapter Five, Jesus/Yeshua is our High Priest and He has atoned for our sins, which included the sin of ignorance. We do not, however, have a license to continue in sin, as emphasized in Hebrews 10:26 and 27: *"For if we sin deliberately after receiving the knowledge of the truth, there no longer remains a sacrifice for sins, but a fearful prospect of judgment..."*

While we're searching the scriptures and on the topic of wisdom and knowledge, one of the most astounding prophecies with clear implications for our day is found in the book of Daniel. *"But you, Daniel, shut up the words, and seal the book, **until the time of the end**. Many shall run to and fro, and knowledge shall increase (Daniel 12:4)."*

Is it not obvious that we live in the prophetic days spoken of by the Prophet Daniel... *"many shall run to and fro, and knowledge shall increase?"*

Never in all of history have human beings been more mobile than they are today, i.e., automobile, air, and space travel (*"running to and fro"*). But what about the words, *"knowledge shall increase"*? The first universities in this country, i.e., Harvard, Yale, Cambridge, etc., were founded as Christian institutions of learning (a matter of historical record)

155

and the Bible was used as the foundation that undergirded knowledge. In all public institutions of learning today, it seems that head knowledge has replaced Bible knowledge. In fact, for all intents and purposes, the Bible has been or is being removed from all public institutions in the United States.

We live today in a culture where communication is so far advanced over anything one could have imagined just a hundred years ago. We can communicate and send information around the world in split seconds. Where information is so available, knowledge is greatly increased. People today are in a state of constant communication with the use of text messaging, Facebook, Twitter, and so many other means of communications. Whether or not that is a good or bad thing is yet to be determined. I suppose it could be a little of both, depending on how it's used. Generally speaking, communication is a good thing. It would certainly be a good thing to learn about and take the time to communicate with our Creator. There are numerous Bible applications and software available online for downloading to computer and mobile devices. Also available are many bible dictionaries and concordances, which are helpful tools in searching out the English meaning of the original Greek and Hebrew text.

Knowledge has exploded so rapidly that it is virtually impossible to keep up. But then, we don't have to! A world of knowledge is available at one's fingertip (not mine...LaVada's) with the click of a "mouse." It's hard to find a creature more lowly than a mouse! A MOUSE is in charge of such KNOWLEDGE?? God tells us that knowledge is going to increase, and it has increased exponentially, and then He puts a little mouse at the controls!

156

"SPARKY, THE SMART MOUSE"

I'm going to leave Sparky, the Smart Mouse, in this updated edition of *TRUTH OR CONSEQUENCES* because I think it illustrates what I'm talking about. Since the first edition in 2009, only six years ago, *Sparky, the Smart Mouse,* might be considered a thing of the past. Now, however, he has an updated "pad." You could say he was hanging on by the tail, but with the advent of the "super mouse" he is losing his tail. Nevertheless, the mouse is still in control! Tail, or no tail!!

Ok, folks, I've got to put this Scripture right here...

"Where is the wise man? Where is the scribe? Where is the debater of this age? Has not God made foolish the wisdom of the world? For since, in the wisdom of God, the world did not know God through wisdom, it pleased God through the folly of what we preach to save those who believe (I Corinthians 1:20-21)*."* And then in Verse 25, Paul says, *"For the foolishness of God is wiser than men, and the weakness of God is stronger than men."*

Now, does God have a sense of humor, or what? Maybe this is coincidence or, maybe He's just trying to tell us something? Why did Paul use the phrase, "the folly of what we preach"? Was it not to emphasize the simplicity of the

157

gospel to those who believe? By the grace of God we are saved through faith in His Word-His Son who went as a lamb to the slaughter voluntarily so that all who believe may be reconciled to God.

When Jesus said, *"It is finished* (John 19:30),"* God had done it all. There is nothing that anyone can "add" to this gospel, which Paul preached that can get one closer to God. All that is necessary is to believe! This "folly" is contrary to the mind of man who so often thinks that he can make himself right with God by what he does. God's gift is complete! How could anything we do make it a better gift, or, how could the doctrines and/or traditions of any church or "religion" make it a better gift? What an incredible gift of love!! There is nothing we can do to repay Him for that gift—BUT, we can love Him back! And how do we do that? We keep His commandments! Jesus said, ***"If you love me, you will keep my commandments*** (John 14:15)."* Then He continues, *"He who has my commandments and keeps them, **he it is who loves me,** and he who loves me will be loved by my Father, and I will love him and manifest myself to him* (John 14:21)."* What an awesome promise!!

Jesus said, *"Think not that I have come to abolish the law and the prophets; I have come not to abolish them but to fulfill them* (Matthew 5:17)."* He then said not even the smallest Hebrew letter or punctuation mark would disappear until all is accomplished. Think about this, Abraham kept the Law[227], Jesus kept the Law[228] and Paul kept the Law.[229] Doesn't it make sense to say that God sent His Son, who lived the Torah (the Law) perfectly and, through His Word and His Spirit, would provide the way for us to *"walk as He walked"* and to live as imitators of Christ? *"He who says he abides in Him*

---

[227] Genesis 26:5
[228] John 15:10
[229] Acts 24:14

ought to walk in the same way in which He walked (1 John 2:6)."

Jesus equipped His disciples to walk as He walked. *"If you love me, you will keep my commandments. And I will pray the Father, to be with you forever, (John 14:15-16)"* *"But the Counselor, the Holy Spirit whom the Father will send in my name, He will teach you all things, and bring to your remembrance all that I have said to you. (John 14:26)"* Jesus taught and lived the Father's word and the Holy Spirit will remind us of His word as we walk as He walked. Demonstrating our love by keeping His commandments should be our goal.

Adam, created in the image of God, failed to walk in obedience when he partook of the tree of knowledge of good and evil after God instructed him not to. So often, what seems to be a little mistake can have big consequences. All of humanity has inherited this condition of disobedience and alienation from God because of Adam's sin. In Christ, God paved the way for a restored relationship and for us to be conformed to His image as we were created to be.

So now we see that what we do is important to God! We are to keep His commandments to demonstrate our love for Jesus and the Father. Faith is made complete by what we do. *"Was not Abraham our Father justified by works, when he offered his son Isaac upon the altar? You see that faith was active along with his works, and faith was completed by works...(James 2:21-22)."* Our works are the result of our gratitude for the gift. Without acknowledging and accepting God's gift, our deeds are but filthy rags.[230] God knows that good works can be accomplished with selfish or evil intent and, therefore, will not only recognize but judge that intent when it does not conform to His Spirit. Everything we do must be in

---

[230] Isaiah 64:6

gratitude for the gift of salvation and there is nothing we can do to earn it.

What does all this mean to a "believing" Christian? A believer's life should be as a walk "down the Emmaus road" where his or her heart and mind is open to the Truth and submissive to the word of God, just as the two disciples who made that trek originally. Luke tells us that Jesus revealed Himself to two disciples on the road to Emmaus as He "opened the scriptures" to them. "Scriptures" here refers to the Torah of Moses, i.e., Genesis, Exodus, Leviticus, Numbers, Deuteronomy, and the Prophets, and the Writings (Psalms, Proverbs, etc.), of the Old Testament. There was no New Testament at that time.[231] Doesn't it make sense to search those "scriptures" in an effort to come to a greater understanding of just who Jesus was and is, rather than referring to them as "Old" and inconsequential, which seems to be the practice in many churches.

Many professing Christians are Christian in name only, that is, they choose to believe what they want to believe about the Bible. Many do not know what the Bible says and, what's more, they don't really care. They truly are as sheep or goats who will follow most anyone who has a message that is pleasing to their ears. Sadly, they may one day hear from the Lord the words, *"Depart from me you who work iniquity."*[232] In my view, this warning is directed at Christians.

Matthew 7:21-23 KJV
Not every one that saith unto me, Lord, Lord, shall enter into the kingdom of heaven; but he that doeth the will of my Father which is in heaven. Many will say to me in that day, Lord, Lord, have we not prophesied in thy name? and in thy name have cast out devils? and in thy name done many wonderful works? And then will I profess unto them, I never

---

[231] Luke 24:13-32
[232] Matthew 7:23 KJV

160

knew you: depart from me, ye that work iniquity.

"Not everyone who says to me, Lord, Lord?" Is it not Christians who call Jesus, "Lord?" This scripture clearly points out that not everyone who calls Him "Lord" will enter the Kingdom, but the ones who <u>do</u> the will of the Father. The word "iniquity" is translated from the Greek word, "*anomia*," which means "lawlessness." The New King James Version translates the word correctly. Those who call themselves Christian while turning away from God's Law should consider this warning.

My prayer is that anyone who is reading this book and fits into this category, will take to heart the scriptural evidence presented in this book and come to the realization that God's prophetic word is **REAL** and it is in effect today just as in the days of Abraham, Moses, the Prophets, Yeshua, and His Disciples.

Proverbs 28:9
If one turns away his ear from hearing the law, even his prayer is an abomination.

Once again, "*sin is the transgression of the law.*"[233] Scripture clearly teaches us that there are consequences for breaking God's Law whether it be intentional or unintentional. On numerous occasions I have heard believers say that they were being attacked by the devil as evidenced by negative consequences going on in their lives. Well... maybe so, or maybe no! Satan was allowed by God to test Job, so perhaps negative circumstances are a test.[234] If there weren't negative consequences for breaking God's commands, how could they be our teacher?[235]

---

[233] 1 John 3:4
[234] Job, Chapter 1
[235] 2 Timothy 3:16

Hebrews 12:5-6

And have you forgotten the exhortation which addresses you as son?[236]*—My son, do not regard lightly the discipline of the Lord,*[237] *nor lose courage when you are punished by Him. For* **the Lord disciplines him who He loves**[238] *and chastises every son whom He receives.*

See also Deuteronomy 8:5, which says the same.

In life we are faced with many choices. When Israel entered the promised land they were given a choice. *"...choose this day whom you will serve...but as for me and my house, we will serve the LORD (Joshua 24:15)."* It is wise to choose God's way.

Although the Bible is filled with prophecy from Genesis to Revelation, very few people seem to take prophecy seriously— ***"for the testimony of Jesus is the Spirit of prophecy*** *(Revelation 19:10)."* It seems to me that all the words that Jesus/Yeshua spoke should be taken seriously. Yeshua said, *"that everything written about me in the Law* [Torah] *of Moses and the Prophets and the Psalms must be fulfilled (Luke 24:44)."* Prophets...Psalms...Torah... That's a lot of prophecy! Prophecy, which would include His second coming. Here I'd like to reemphasize what Yeshua/Jesus said in the Gospel of Luke. *"And He said to them, 'O foolish men, and slow of heart to believe all that the prophets have spoken ... (Luke 24:25)!"* Yeshua himself is telling us directly to believe all that the prophets have spoken. Doesn't it make sense to follow His instructions?

---

[236] Proverbs 3:11-12
[237] Job 5:17
[238] Psalm 94:12; 119:67, 75; Revelations 3:19

$$\ast\ast\ast\ast$$

One last personal note…

As a child growing up on a farm, my grandparent's house was only about a minute's walk away from our house. My dad and grandpa raised poultry and plowed about 150 acres of land, which had been in the family since 1897. They also ran sheep and cattle along with milk cows on about another 150 acres. For years they did the plowing with a couple of plow horses and a single row plow. Can you imagine walking behind a couple of plow horses for days and plowing that much land? In 1936, Dad bought a new Farmall tractor and a two-row plow. I wasn't on the scene yet, but I can just imagine the excitement when Dad cranked that tractor for the first time and started turning that ground at least six to eight times as fast as before! I actually cranked that tractor (no battery or starter) a few times and plowed a few acres of that farm in later years.

Cranking that tractor wasn't nearly as exciting as when my "Oma" cranked the handle on that wall telephone for the first time to talk to a neighbor. I am not sure of the year when that happened, but I can still remember my grandmother standing there in the foyer of the old home place holding the black bell-shaped receiver to her ear and speaking into the mouthpiece of that old wooden telephone box on the wall. She would be happily carrying on a "long distance" conversation in German with Mrs. Heimer, who lived about two miles up the road. Today we think nothing about traveling Interstate 10 at 80 mph in West Texas carrying on a conversation with anyone, anywhere in the world, on our cell phone. It is now common to not only carry on a conversation but to actually see the person to whom you are speaking, when you have the right equipment.

What a tremendous advancement in communication and technology in just two generations!

Many improvements have been made in communications technology just since the first edition of this book in 2009, e.g., visual communication via Skype, FaceTime, etc. About a year ago, my wife and I visited family via the internet while they were vacationing in France and recently, while they were vacationing in Argentina. We could see them perfectly and there was no delay in our voice communication. We also visited a pastor friend in India via Skype. This and other technology, such as GPS, and much more, is now available on smart phones, tablets, etc. There seems to be almost no end to the advancement in technology. By the time a product is on the market, something new, faster and better, has been developed. For people like us, in our generation, who can remember party lines, telegraph, and something called "snail mail," all this is pretty remarkable. But to young people who have been born into this age, it seems to be quite ordinary. It's really not ordinary, it's prophecy fulfilled! *"...Many shall run to and fro, and knowledge shall increase* (Daniel 12:4).*"*

CHAPTER FOURTEEN

PETER, PAUL AND PROPHECY

II Peter 1:19

And we have the <u>prophetic word</u> made more sure. You will do well to <u>pay attention</u> to this as to a lamp shining in a dark place...

II Peter 1:20-21

First of all you must understand this, that no prophecy of scripture is a matter of one's own interpretation, because no prophecy ever came by the impulse of man, but men moved by the Holy Spirit spoke from God.

Later in this epistle, Peter warns of false prophets and teachers who by their own interpretation of Scripture will bring destructive heresies and cause many to follow their licentiousness which is to use God's grace as a license to sin. *"But false prophets also arose among the people, just as there will be false teachers among you, who will secretly bring in destructive heresies, even denying the Master who bought them, bringing upon themselves swift destruction. And many will follow their licentiousness, and because of them the way of truth will be reviled (2 Peter 2:1-2)."*

Unfortunately, there are false teachers in many churches today. My prayer would be for God to be merciful and call them to repentance.

"Forsaking the right way they [the prophets and teachers] *have gone astray; they have followed the way of Balaam, the son of Be´or, who loved gain from wrongdoing, but was rebuked for his own transgression; a dumb ass spoke with human voice and restrained the prophet's madness* (II Peter 2:15-16).*"* Do you remember the Balaam I introduced you to in the foreword of this book? It's the same dude! Peter continues to warn of prophets and teachers and their methods…

II Peter 2:19
They promised them freedom, but they themselves are **slaves of corruption***; for whatever overcomes a man, to that he is enslaved.*

II Peter 3:3-4
First of all you must understand this, that scoffers will come in the last days with scoffing, following their own passions and saying, "Where is the promise of His coming? For ever since the fathers fell asleep, [died] *all things have continued as they were in the beginning of creation.*

Once more, Peter uses "first of all" to get the reader's attention. The inference here is "you'd better get this!" Jude, the brother of James and Jesus, also points to "scoffers" in the last days, mockers who are ungodly people perverting the Grace of God into licentiousness. (Jude, verses 4 and 18.) Have you ever come across anyone with this attitude? If we could only comprehend God's "time" and timing…

II Peter 3:8-9

But do not ignore this one fact, beloved, that with the Lord one day is as a thousand years, and a thousand years as one day. The Lord is not slow about His promise as some count slowness, but is forbearing toward you, not wishing that any should perish, but that all should reach repentance.

Peter is reminding us of God's compassion and patience but he is also admonishing us to repent and walk in the way of the Messiah. So, should we live in fear? Absolutely not! *"For God hath not given us the **spirit of fear**; but of power, and of love, and of a sound mind (II Timothy 1:7 KJV)."* When the Holy Spirit resides in us, the fear of what is going on around us is removed. God is love! Perfect love casts out fear.[239]

The underlying message of prophecy is to believe and be prepared spiritually for His return. That's the message of the maidens and their lamps in Matthew 25:1-13. Five were foolish and five were wise. The wise came with extra oil for their lamps. The foolish maidens ran out of oil for their lamps and thus, were not prepared for Messiah's return. Don't get caught in the situation where there is no oil for your lamp. His word is the oil, or the "fuel" for the lamp, which lights our way. *"Thy word is a lamp to my feet and a light to my path* (Psalm 119:105).*"*

God's word assures us of the security we have when we seek God with all our heart and the salvation we have by grace through faith in Jesus Christ. While referring to the last days, God's word admonishes us in Joel 2:12, *"Even now, says the Lord, return to me with all your heart..."* What an awesome and merciful God!

---

[239] I John 4:18

To prepare us for Messiah's return, Paul tells us…

I Thessalonians 4:16-17

For the Lord himself will descend from heaven with a shout, with the archangel's call, and with the sound of the trumpet of God. And the dead in Christ will rise first; then we who are alive, who are left, shall be caught up together with them in the clouds to meet the Lord in the air…

It seems that in various corners of Christianity there is dissension on what this business of "being caught up" is all about. Being caught up is what the word "rapture" refers to; and this word *rapture* is not in the English Bible. It is, however, in the Latin Vulgate, which was in use for about 1300 years. The phrase, "caught up" is translated from the Greek word, *harpazo,* and the Latin word, *rapere.*[240] Many argue as to when this will happen. (Pre/Mid/Post-Tribulation)

For me, scripture seems to be quite clear. Concerning the end of the age, Jesus was asked by His disciples, *"tell us when this will be and what will be the sign of your coming and of the close of the age (Matthew 24:3)?"* Jesus responded that many would be led astray and that believers would hear of wars, rumors of wars, famines and earthquakes, etc., and that they would be delivered up to tribulation and hated for the sake of His name.[241]

Later in this chapter, He says, ***"Immediately after the tribulation of those days** the sun will be darkened, and the moon will not give its light, and the stars will fall from heaven, and the powers of the heavens will be shaken; **then will appear the sign of the Son of Man** in heaven, and then all the tribes of the earth will mourn, and **they will see the Son of Man coming***

---

[240] David Humpal, Study of the End Time, Accessed 9/1/08
http://www.elite.net/~ebedyah/PastorsSite/weeklystudies/questionsalways/study8.htm
[241] Matthew 24:4-9

168

in the clouds of heaven with power and great glory;* (Matthew 24:29-30).”

Please note that immediately after the tribulation of those days they will see the Son of Man coming in the clouds! This is in sharp contrast to the *Left Behind* book and movie series! Those who believe and teach the pre-tribulation rapture should ask the Christians in Egypt, Syria, and Iraq, what their thoughts are on the matter? Christians there have faced unbelievable tribulation… persecution, torture, and death. We should all pray for these Christians. But in addition, we should stand up and speak out to the leaders of our nation who have the power to provide assistance and refuge.

Perhaps more important than the rapture disagreement is the question, are we ready for His return? Are you? If He comes tomorrow?? You should realize that someday He will come today! Paul tells us, in I Thessalonians 5:2-6, *“For you yourselves know well that the day of the Lord will come like a thief in the night. When people say, 'there is peace and security,' then sudden destruction will come upon them as travail comes upon a woman with child, and there will be no escape.* **But you are not in darkness, brethren, for that day to surprise you like a thief**. *For you are all sons of light and sons of the day; we are not of the night or of darkness. So then let us not sleep as others do, but let us keep awake and be sober.”*

Note that Paul reminds the “brethren” that they are not in darkness and that they are not to be surprised. So, as children of the light (believers), we should watch and stay sober so as to not be caught unaware. Then he assures us in Chapter 5:9, *“For God has not destined us for wrath, but to obtain salvation through our Lord Jesus Christ.”*

Consider also Moses made a prophetic observation about the latter days and the tribulation when he told Israel about the consequence for disobedience and for forgetting their covenant with God.

Deuteronomy 4:27-31

And the LORD will scatter you among the peoples, and you will be left few in number among the nations where the LORD will drive you. ...But from there you will seek the LORD your God, and you will find Him, if you search after Him with all your heart and with all your soul. **When you are in tribulation,** *and all these things come upon you* **in the latter days***, you will return to the LORD your God and obey His voice, for the LORD your God is a merciful God; He will not fail you or destroy you or forget the covenant with your fathers which He swore to them.*

Note that at the time of this prophecy Israel was still one nation. The northern kingdom had not yet been divorced and scattered. This prophecy was addressed to all the tribes of Israel and it seems that in the latter days they would be included in tribulation.

Now, what does all this mean to the nonbeliever? Well, my prayer is that after reading this book, God has touched you in such a way so that you are no longer in this category. If you are not yet convinced, then I would ask you to compare the words of the Bible to the teaching of anyone who has ever come up with what they think is a path to God. Perhaps you have been wondering about and searching for that path and are a bit confused by what seems to be a myriad of paths that point in different directions.

From where do all the various "religions of the world" come? These religions may take the form of worshipping manmade objects, worshipping some part of creation, i.e., the sun or moon, but what is perhaps most common is the worship, or veneration, of a **non-biblical Jesus** which is to use the Name of Jesus but twist His teaching or deny His deity. These religions are all the culmination of man's attempt to find God, or invent a god according to one's idea of who one thinks God is, or a god that may be a bit more accessible, visible, compassionate, or powerful. A god, or idol—from where we get the word *idolatry*—can be anyone or anything to which a person gives first priority or allegiance, i.e., money, career, "grown-up toys", movie or sports stars, etc. If the God of the Bible is to be your God, He must be put first!

Understandably, to lump all religions together attempting to define or explain each in a single paragraph could honestly be considered a bit simplistic. To explain or delve into each of them extensively would take more than one book, more time than I have, and would obscure the message I am trying to convey. Although I have limited knowledge of the various religions, I do have a little understanding of the fundamentals and the history of some of them. My intent is not to offend persons of another faith, but to encourage the reader to compare and examine whether or not what I have said about the God of the Bible is true.

The God of the Bible is exclusive and He doesn't beat around the bush. *"I am God and there is no other...*(Isaiah 46:9)."* In Exodus 20:5-6, He tells us, *"...I the Lord your God am a jealous God, visiting the iniquity of the fathers upon the children to the third and the fourth generation of those who hate me, but showing steadfast love to thousands of those who love me and keep my commandments."* After all, why would the Creator of the Universe find it necessary to share His glory with imposters? He alone deserves our love and adoration as Creator. Think about it!

Jesus said that no one gets to the Father except through Him.[242] This again is very exclusive! After all, if God is who He says He is, and I believe He is, He doesn't need me or

---

[242] John 14:6

anyone else to defend Him. He simply calls to all who have ears to hear: *"Come now, and let us reason together," says the LORD", Though your sins are like scarlet, they shall be as white as snow; Though they are red like crimson, They shall be as wool.* (Isaiah 1:18)" God challenges us to check Him out. By His grace, His word brings life to our inner being (soul) to the point where we can respond in faith. In faith, we acknowledge Yeshua/Jesus as the Son of God and 'repent' —turn away from sin and our worldly ways, to God's ways— then watch as our sins become as "white as snow" and the burden associated with them disappears.

Now, how does God accomplish this? Yeshua was without sin.[243] And, as such, became our sacrificial lamb—our Passover Lamb! When we sin and repent, we are covered by His shed blood. His gift according to His grace. All that is required is real repentance and real submission to His word. God's grace does not give us permission or a license to willingly continue in sin. What is sin? Sin is the transgression of the Law, which is Torah.[244] Yeshua told the woman caught in adultery, *"Go and sin no more."*[245]

Colossians 3:5-10
Put to death therefore what is earthly in you: fornication, impurity, passion, evil desire, and covetousness, which is idolatry. On account of these the wrath of God is coming. In these you once walked, when you lived in them. But now put them all away: anger, wrath, malice, slander, and foul talk from your mouth. Do not lie to one another, seeing that you have put off the old nature with its practices and have put on the new nature, which is being renewed in knowledge after the image of its creator.

---

[243] Hebrews 4:15
[244] 1 John 3:4
[245] John 8:11

If all the people in the world who profess Christianity would practice and live up to the instructions in this one scripture, can you imagine the profound impact this would have on the world in which we live? We are all sinners, and I confess that I could say, like Paul, that I am chief among sinners![246] God prefers that we would all come to repentance.[247]

Paul gave us reasons for the coming wrath of God. The first being fornication, which for all intents and purposes is accepted as normal behavior in our contemporary American culture. Fornication is all sex outside of the biblical definition of marriage. Apparently, few, if any, preachers in this nation are preaching on this sin because it is as common within the culture of those inside the church as well as those outside the church. Fornication is the primary cause of abortion, which has grown into an industry that has taken the lives of millions of innocent babies. Also, the consequential curse associated with transgressing this law of God is the root cause for divorce, which again is about as common for the 'churched' as it is for the 'unchurched.' With sin comes curse—the evidence is before our eyes!

Romans 6:16
Do you not know that if you yield yourselves to anyone as obedient slaves, you are slaves of the one whom you obey, either of sin, which leads to death, or of obedience, which leads to righteousness?

Paul has a masterful way of contrasting *sin* and *obedience...* and, he says we are slaves to either one or the other. As I pointed out in the beginning of this chapter, Peter warned of false prophets who by their interpretation of Scripture would use God's grace as a license to sin.[248] In light

---

[246] 1 Timothy 1:15 KJV
[247] 2 Peter 3:9
[248] 2 Peter 2:1-3

of this scripture, why would a loving father give us a "license to sin" which leads to death? Doesn't make sense! Does it?

Long before Paul wrote any of his letters, Moses recorded that it was "for our good" that we should follow God's instructions and keep His commandments.

Deuteronomy 10:12-13
*And now, Israel, what does the LORD your God require of you, but to fear the LORD your God, to walk in all His ways, to love Him, to serve the LORD your God with all your heart and with all your soul, and to keep the commandments and statutes of the LORD, which I command you this day **for your good**?*

And how does one go about finding this God of the Bible? God has the answer in his word recorded long ago. His word holds true today.

Jeremiah 29:13
You will seek me and find me, when you seek me with all your heart.

Deuteronomy 4:29
...you will seek the Lord your God, and you will find Him, if you search after Him with all your heart and with all your soul.

Matthew 7:7
Ask and it will be given to you, seek and you will find, knock and the door will be opened to you.

Revelation 3:20
Behold, I [Jesus] stand at the door and knock; if anyone hears my voice and opens the door, I will come into him and eat with him, and he with me.

174

PROVERBS

3:5-6 (NIV) *Trust in the Lord with all your heart and lean not on your own understanding. In all your ways acknowledge Him and He will make your paths straight.*

8:17 *I love those who love me and those who seek me diligently find me.*

8:32 *And now my sons, listen to me; happy are those who keep my ways.*

8:35-36 (NIV) *"For whoever finds me finds life and receives favor from the LORD. But whoever fails to find me harms himself; all who hate me love death."*

Deuteronomy 7:9
...God keeps covenant and steadfast love with those who love Him and keep His commandments to a thousand generations.

God has given us his "Word," Yeshua, to emulate and follow. If we truly are in His "Word," His "Word" will live in us. *"There is therefore now no condemnation for those who are in Christ Jesus (Romans 8:1)."* God does not condemn us. He looks at us through the blood of Yeshua. If we feel condemnation, we should look at our own being. Have we committed our lives to be a reflection of His word and His love? If we have committed our life to Messiah, we will no longer be able to sin without feeling the conviction of the Holy Spirit. Out with the old and in with the new! We are a new creation! And if our life does not reflect that change, perhaps we should examine our commitment. Let's just be honest. He sees all, hears all, and knows all. And, He knows you!

When your heart is ready, you don't even have to look. God examines the mind and heart of each person who comes to Him —individually—not corporately. God has no grandchildren—only children! When you're ready to repent and submit to His authority, all you have to do is ask. Come as you are. Yeshua alone has the power to change lives and that includes yours! You won't be able to see Him and you won't be able to touch Him, but you will know He has touched you! You'll know that He lives in you. The "Light of the World" is available personally for all who long for and seek Him with all their heart. If all of this is starting to make sense to you, you may ask yourself, now what? The answer is, according to scripture, repent and be baptized. Afterwards, find yourself a group, or assembly, of believers who are sincerely searching for Truth and are looking to imitate the church in the Book of Acts!

With regard to the authenticity of the Bible, no writing in the history of antiquity is so well documented. None can compare! The *Septuagint*, a Greek translation of the Hebrew Old Testament, dates to about 200 B.C. There are over 24,000 copies of various New Testament writings, written from the time period 40-100 A.D. with copies that date to as early as 125 A.D. Josh MacDowell, the author of the book, *Evidence That Demands a Verdict*[249] does a good job of documenting the evidence for the Bible's authenticity. In addition, the Dead Sea Scrolls, found in eleven caves in Qumran, Israel, in 1947, include the oldest complete copy of the Book of Isaiah, which verifies that the words of Isaiah recorded in our Bibles today are identical to the words recorded then. Coincidentally, 1947 was the year that the United Nations voted to allow Israel to become a nation. Coincidentally??

The fact that the words of the Bible's Old Testament we read today are the same words that were quoted and read by

---

[249] Evidence That Demands a Verdict, by Josh MacDowell, Published by Here's Life Publishers, Inc., 1979, Campus Crusade for Christ, Inc.

Yeshua and His disciples in the Temple of Jerusalem 2000 years ago is a witness to the fact that God has protected His word through the ages. This, by itself, is reason enough to trust that the word of God is true, and can and should be used as a standard to determine truth. You can add to that, "proof by prophetic word" because so much that God has prophesied has already happened. We can rest assured that prophecy which has not yet happened is happening today and will happen in the future until all is fulfilled. **That's right! God has given us "prophecy" to prove Himself!** No other god has prophesied specific future events centuries before they happened. He challenged them through the prophet Isaiah roughly twenty-eight hundred years ago.

Isaiah 41:21-24

*Set forth your case, says the Lord; bring your proofs, says the king of Jacob. Let them bring them, and tell us what is to happen. Tell us the former things, what they are, that we may consider them, that we may know their outcome; or declare to us the things to come. Tell us what is to come hereafter, **that we may know you are gods;** do good, or do harm, that we may be dismayed and terrified. Behold, you are nothing, and your work is naught; an abomination is he who chooses you.*

No god has ever accepted that challenge! The reason: no god except the God of Creation is eternal, knows all, and lives yesterday, today, and forever.[250] No other god is the true God!

The fulfillment of God's prophecies is certain and "is happening" in our time while those in the world, as in the days of Lot and as in the days of Noah float along in a tide of indifference or outright rebellion.

---

[250] Hebrews 13:8

Luke 17:26-30

*As it was in the days of Noah, so will it be in the days of the Son of Man.   They ate, they drank, they married, they were given in marriage, until the day when Noah entered the ark, and the flood came and destroyed them all.   Likewise, as it was in the days of Lot—they ate, they drank, they bought, they sold, they planted, they built, but on the day when Lot went out from Sodom fire and brimstone rained from heaven and destroyed them all—**so will it be on the day when the Son of Man is revealed.***

To look at our culture in light of the U.S. Supreme Court decision on June 26, 2015, to legalize same-sex marriage, this scripture should be enough reason for anyone to pause and reflect.   Wouldn't it be great if our Supreme Court Justices would take a walk down the Emmaus Road!

CHAPTER FIFTEEN

ON THE ROAD TO EMMAUS

God said to Abraham and his descendants:

Genesis 12:3 NKJV
I will bless those who bless you, And I will curse him who curses you; And in you all the families of the earth shall be blessed.

Then He said to Abraham's son, Isaac:

Genesis 26:4-5
I will multiply your descendants as the stars in heaven, and will give your descendants all these lands; and by your descendants **all the nations of the earth shall bless themselves**: *because Abraham obeyed my voice and kept my charge, my commandments, my statutes, and my laws.*

Please note that Abraham obeyed God's voice and kept God's commandments, statutes and laws long before the Law was given to Moses at Mt. Sinai. The blessings and promises of God to Abraham were the consequence of his obedience.

Because of Abraham's obedience, God's purpose for Israel was to bless all earthly families. Could it be that God has been doing that over the centuries and the world is simply unaware? Could it be that when God divorced the northern ten tribes of Israel and scattered them throughout the world, He used it as part of His plan to keep His promise to Abraham and, thus, to fulfill His purpose? *"...by your descendents all the nations of the earth shall bless themselves (Genesis 26:5)."*

Jeremiah 3:8

She [Judah] *saw that for all the adulteries of that faithless one, Israel, I have sent her away with a decree of divorce; yet her false sister Judah did not fear, but she too went and played the harlot.*

Jeremiah records that God divorced Israel and sent her away. Judah, however, was not divorced even though she, too, played the harlot. Why? Perhaps because the Jewish people were responsible for keeping the oracles of God.[251] Remember from the brief history review in Chapter 2 that the northern kingdom of Israel was also referred to as "Ephraim." This divorce resulted in the dispersion of the ten tribes. The Letter of James, the brother of Yeshua, was addressed to the twelve tribes, which would have included the ten tribes of Ephraim and the two tribes of Judah. *"James, a servant of God and of the Lord Jesus Christ, to the twelve tribes in the dispersion: Greetings (James 1:1)."* [Side Note of trivia: Yeshua's brother's name was Ya'akov in Hebrew and should be translated as Jacob in English, but was translated as "James" in the King James Bible.]

Peter's first epistle was also addressed to the *"exiles of the dispersion."*[252] God knew then as well as today where His exiles were and are! He has been scattering blessings around the world for centuries and the world is oblivious. The nation of Judah has been scattered all over the world and, in general, the Jewish people have been persecuted wherever they went, and yet they have been a blessing to the nations.

Jews currently make up approximately 0.25% or, one-fourth of one percent of the world's population and 2% of the

---

[251] Romans 3:2
[252] I Peter 1:1

U.S. population.[253] The Nobel Prize was established in Alfred Nobel's will in 1895 and was first awarded in 1901. Between 1901 and 2007, 27% of worldwide recipients and 40% of U.S. recipients in the scientific and research fields of Chemistry, Economics, Medicine and Physics were Jewish or persons of half-Jewish ancestry. In other words, worldwide, the Jewish people, outnumbered by four hundred to one, received more than one out of every four of these awards, and in the U. S., outnumbered by fifty to one, received two out of every five of the awards in these various research fields. That's 25%+ worldwide and 40% in the U.S.! Advances in these research fields are fundamental to the advancement of western civilization. A list of Nobel recipients is posted in Appendix A at the end of this chapter.

Perhaps a reason for these outstanding and incredibly lopsided achievements in these various research fields is that many fathers in traditional Jewish families speak God's blessings over their children every Sabbath. The world would be a much better place if we all spoke words of encouragement and God's blessings over our children. So many children never feel the love of a father and, as a result, may be handicapped in the development of their God-given talents and gifts.

So, why does the world reject the Jewish people and the blessings of God? I believe it is because the world is deceived by that **spirit who is the father of lies**! America was founded as a Christian nation. This is well documented.[254] The United States Government, however, seems to be increasingly hostile to both Jews and Christians. From our nation's very beginnings, America has generally been a haven and friend to the Jewish people. I think I can safely say that no other nation

---

[253] JINFO.ORG - http://www.jinfo.org/index.html

[254] WallBuilders, LLC, PO Box 397 Aledo, TX 76008, (http://www.wallbuilders.com/default.asp).

in history has received more of God's favor than the United States of America. Other nations are blessed with great resources and wonderful people and yet are not as blessed as this nation, which I believe, is the direct result of America's Christian foundation and its friendship with the descendants of Abraham, Isaac, and Jacob. Christopher Columbus, a likely Jewish descendant, came to America by divine providence and opened the door to a nation where Christians and Jews could prosper and live together in peace.

Today very few people are knowledgeable about American history and even fewer know anything about the history of Israel. Most Americans are unaware of the basis for our Judeo-Christian heritage. In 1975, a United States postal stamp honored a Jewish man named Haym Salomon for his contribution to America's freedom. [255] Salomon was a merchant banker and personal friend of George Washington. He devoted his life and fortune as well as expertise raising money abroad to finance the American Revolution. He made loans to the newly formed American government and most of these loans were never repaid. Without his contribution, the American Revolution would almost surely have failed. Other Jews, including a militia company known as the "Jews Company", from South Carolina, fought alongside American patriots to win our coveted freedoms. [256] Today freedom, which is so often taken for granted, is being eroded at an alarming pace.

Christianity and Israel are increasingly under persecution and attack around the world. As Christians and Americans, we should stand with Israel, as a nation and as a people. Jews and Christians have a common link to the patriarchs, Abraham, Isaac and Jacob, in our Jewish Messiah. Many Jewish people have already come to the knowledge of Yeshua as the Messiah and, in God's time as clearly prophesied in His word, so will

---

[255] Jewish Voice Today, July/August 2005
[256] Ibid.

the remainder of all Israel.[257]   According to Psalm 122:6, we should pray for the peace of Jerusalem! This word "peace" is translated from the Hebrew word "*shalom*" which means more than just the absence of hostility, but also includes the blessings of health, wellbeing, comfort, success, contentment, and to be made whole and complete. *Shalom* is commonly used as a greeting in Israel and *shalom* should be our prayer for Israel as well.

I hope this book will inspire you to spend a little time in His word *(the sword of the Spirit)* because personal Bible study is of utmost importance. How are we to know if someone is leading us down a path of "untruth" which is so often the reason for those stumbling blocks in life? When it comes to truth, don't take my word or anyone else's as "gospel" but examine for yourself what is true.[258] Put on the whole armor of God and stand your ground "defending the faith" in these "latter days."[259] The consequences and rewards are eternal!! As one passionate Hebrew Roots teacher says, "Go home and read your Bible!"[260]

Most everyone would agree that the Bible is not all that easy to read and understand. The Bible is a spiritual book and cannot be comprehended intellectually. To receive even a hint of the Truth it contains, one must submit to the possibility that it is the Word of God. Hebrews 11:6 tells us that, *"And without faith it is impossible to please Him. For **whoever would draw near to God must believe that He exists** and that He rewards those who seek Him."* I cannot comprehend why the Bible is written the way it is but I know that God prefers obedience and requires faith if we want to be close to Him.

---

[257] Romans 11:26
[258] Acts 17:11
[259] Ephesians 6:14-17
[260] Zachary Bauer, *New2Torah Ministries, http://new2torah.com*

Two things the Bible makes very clear are: God's incredible love for and devotion to man (mankind) and His faithfulness to His word. He loves the Church and He loves Israel. There is no separation between those who are "grafted in" to the same tree.[261] The Church referred to as *The Way* or *the assembly* in Scripture is made up of all who repent and believe the Gospel…a people who are called out and set apart to be a witness to His word. It's not about who has the biggest building or what name is on that building. God is not into marketing "brand" names. Paul tells us in I Corinthians 1:10 there should not be quarreling and dissensions among believers and that they should be united in the same mind. Then he says, *"What I mean is that each one of you says, 'I belong to Paul,' or 'I belong to Apol'los,' or 'I belong to Cephas,'* [Peter] *or 'I belong to Christ.'"* He goes on to ask, *"Is Christ divided?"*[262] I realize Paul is speaking about individuals in the church at Corinth, but couldn't these words just as well apply today to the church at large? Couldn't we just as well say here, "I belong to the Methodist" or, "I belong to the Baptist" or, "I belong to the Catholic," or, "I belong to the Lutheran, Church of Christ, Presbyterian, Episcopal, Cowboy, or *Whatever* Christian Church?"

Wherever we are, we should be reflecting His light. Every believer is called to be a witness to the Truth. And, churches should not be engaged in competition! One body, one Spirit! *"There is one body and one Spirit, just as you were called to the one hope that belongs to your call, one Lord, one faith, one baptism, one God and Father of us all, who is above all and through all and in all* (Ephesians 4:4-6)." What I am saying is people need to understand that it is not the name above the door of your church that will prepare anyone for the Kingdom of God or save a single soul. What Paul is saying is that there

---

[261] Galatians 3:28
[262] 1 Corinthians 1:12-13

184

is only one name that matters... the NAME ABOVE ALL NAMES, YESHUA/JESUS!![263]

Perhaps it's time to take a look at the very word, *church*, which seems to have taken on a connotation of a building or a place rather than an assembly of believers. Many people tend to place their allegiance to a church or denomination rather than to the Word of God. As a result, people who "go to" *church* have become what might be referred to as "flavor seekers" rather than "Truth seekers." Just choose your flavor! The word *church*, is the King James translation of the Greek word, *ecclesia*, which in turn was the translation of the Hebrew word *kahal*. A more accurate translation of this word *ecclesia* would be *congregation* or *assembly*.[264] *Ecclesia* means a called out body or set apart assembly of believers. Israel was referred to as a congregation, or assembly, i.e., church, when they received the Law at Mt. Sinai. *"This is that Moses who said to the children of Israel, 'The LORD your God will raise up for you a Prophet like me from your brethren. Him you shall hear.' This is he who was in **the congregation** [ekklesia] in the wilderness with the Angel who spoke to him on Mt Sinai, and with our fathers, the one who received the living oracles to give to us (Acts 7:37-38)."*

You can drive through Anytown, USA, and there is a "church" on practically every corner. In bigger cities, churches are a little bigger and a little bit further apart. There is a church of almost any flavor...kind of like Baskin-Robbins. In many of these churches, there are dedicated preachers who seek and preach the "truth" according to their understanding of God's word. Others have preachers who accommodate "the itching ears" of their parishioners and preach unbiblical half-truths because that is what the people want to hear. Never mind what the Bible says... They say, "That was just for those heathens in years gone by." or "We know so much more now than they

---

[263] Acts 4:12
[264] *Strong's Concordance*, #1577 - *ecclesia*

knew then." or, "Those stories are just myths or allegories." or, "Where is the promise of His coming? Aren't things the same as they've always been?" They have, in effect, created a god unto their own imagination, who is powerless and not at all representative of the Truth, which is God's Word. They have not taken into account Peter's word. *"The Lord is not slow about His promise as some count slowness, but is forbearing toward you, not wishing that any should perish, but that all should reach repentance (2 Peter 3:9)."*

The further the Church strays from the Truth that is the Word of God, the greater the division. Listen to the words of Jesus in John 17 as He prayed for the disciples when the time for His crucifixion was drawing near. *"And this is eternal life, that they may know You, the only true God, and Jesus Christ whom You have sent (John 17:3 NKJV)."* How can we know the true God without knowing and keeping His word? *"Now by this we know that we know Him, if we keep His commandments. He who says, "I know Him," and does not keep His commandments, is a liar, and the truth is not in him. But whoever keeps His word, truly the love of God is perfected in him. By this we know that we are in Him.(1 John 2:3-5 NKJV)"*

Jesus continues to pray for His disciples, *"They are not of the world, just as I am not of the world. Sanctify them by Your truth. Your word is truth. As You sent Me into the world, I also have sent them into the world. (John 17:16-18 NKJV)."* Sanctify means to set apart as holy or for holy purposes; to consecrate.[265] In other words, His disciples are to be set apart in His Word which is Truth for His holy purposes. Then Jesus prays for those who will believe in Him (the church or assembly) through the word of His disciples.

---

[265] Funk & Wagnals New Comprehensive International Dictionary of the English Language, Encyclopedic Edition, J. G. Ferguson Publishing, 1980

John 17:20-23 NKJV

*I do not pray for these alone, but also for those who will believe in Me through their word; that **they all may be one**, as You, Father, are in Me, and I in You; that they also may be one in Us, **that the world may believe** that You sent Me. And the glory which You gave Me I have given them, that they may be one just as We are one: I in them, and You in Me; that they may be made perfect in one, and **that the world may know** that You have sent Me, and have loved them as You have loved Me.*

Because of the division, which is so apparent in the Church, one can only imagine what the Christian Church must look like to non-believers. Jesus' prayer was that the Church **would become one!** Why? So **that the world may believe!** So **that the world may know!** — That Jesus was sent to demonstrate the love of God! Looking at church history, I believe you would have to admit that this prayer was much needed and that the Church, so far, has failed to be made perfect in one and to know and believe that He sent Yeshua for this purpose. Why the failure? It's because we stray from the Truth while following the doctrines and traditions of men. If it's the Truth that **"sets us free,"** then it stands to reason that **lies keep us in bondage**. Unity can and will only come by being sanctified in Truth. It's time for the people of the Church to repent of any teaching not grounded in God's word and watch as He heals the Body with His mercy and grace. (The word, *repent,* which is translated from the Hebrew word, *teshuva,* simply means to turn around and walk in God's way. In other words, keep His commandments and follow His instructions, the Torah.)

Jesus said, *"If you love me, you will keep my commandments (John 14:15)."* Which commandments do you suppose He was talking about? *"If you keep My commandments, you will abide in My love, just as I have kept My Father's commandments and abide in His love (John 15:10 NKJV)."* Does it make sense that He would exclude some of His Father's commandments, which He said that He kept?

187

That's not at all likely! Since Yeshua was with God and was the Word of God, "in the beginning,"[266] would it not stand to reason that He was speaking of all commandments "from the beginning?" He also said, *"A new commandment I give to you, that you love one another; even as I have loved you, that you also love one another.* ***By this all men will know that you are my disciples, if you have love for one another*** (John 13:34-35). *"*

If you have love for one another!! Looks like we fail in this category, too. Forgiveness is an ordained consequence of love and love is an ordained consequence of forgiveness. Can we not see the importance of forgiveness? Can we comprehend the importance of love? Can we begin to comprehend the importance of "being one"? Can we comprehend the importance of Truth? **Without being sanctified in Truth, we can never reach that place where we are sanctified in His love.** Forgive, be patient in love, but never compromise the Word who is Truth! If the Truth is compromised, it can no longer be considered Truth. The "father" of lies knows that even one lie successfully planted causes division in the Body of Christ.

When Yeshua was asked which is the greatest commandment in the Law, He responded, *"You shall love the Lord your God with all your heart, and with all your soul, and with all your mind. This is the great and first commandment. And a second is like it, 'You shall love your neighbor as yourself.' On these two commandments* ***depend all the Law and the Prophets*** (Matthew 22:37-40). *"* To depend on does not mean to depart from! All of God's commandments are given for us to show our love of God and love for our neighbor. Accordingly, if we fail to love our neighbor, we have failed in keeping God's Law/Torah!

---

[266] John 1:1

The Christian practice of following the traditions of men over the instructions in God's Word causes division in the body of Christ and is a deterrent to taking the Gospel to the "Jew first." Thus, the consequence of this practice is a perpetuation of the division in all those who profess to believe in and follow the God of Abraham, Isaac, and Jacob. (Jews and Christians) Isn't it time to pray for God to heal this division as only He can? Thy Kingdom come, Thy Will be done! Amen !

The people of Israel are the covenant people physically descended from Abraham who was considered righteous because of his faith.[267] This covenant of righteousness through faith was passed on to Isaac and Jacob. The evidence of scriptural references contained herein, plus recent history, and current events make it clear that God has a plan for this people and that He is steadfast in accomplishing His plan and purpose to bring them home and cleanse them in the process of giving them a "heart transplant."[268]

Why would God have to choose or favor the Church over Israel, or vice versa? The fact is that He doesn't have to and His word clearly says He's not going to! God is almighty and His love is big enough to include both the Church and Israel and then some! Why do we try to limit God by putting Him in a box that will never be able to contain Him? —FOR GOD SO LOVED THE WORLD— He is big enough and has the power to accomplish His plan and purpose for both, and I believe that, in the end, both will become one in Him. Those grafted into the same tree are one tree and are sanctified and made righteous by the shared root, i.e., the "root of Jesse" which is Yeshua the Messiah. In the end, they will be one and the same. A **set apart people**, an *ecclesia,* a congregation of believers in the one true God. A *"one new man"* assembly of Jew and Gentile believers… Israel.

---

[267] Romans 4:3
[268] Clifton Jansky Ministries, http://www.cliftonjansky.com -- Thanks, CJM!

When true believers in the Church come to realize their true identity in Israel and accept Judah as their brother, and likewise the people of Judah come to recognize and accept these Christians as their brother Joseph (Ephraim), then I believe God will begin the healing process of making us, Jew and Gentile, one in Him.[269] The Apostle Paul tells us, *"there is neither Jew nor Greek, there is neither slave nor free, there is neither male nor female; for you are all one in Christ Jesus. And if you are Christ's, then you are Abraham's offspring, heirs according to promise* (Galatians 3:28-29)."

As the end of this age draws near, it is not necessary to understand the why of God's plan and purpose for Israel or the Church, but it is to our benefit to accept and submit to it. Whether or not we do that, however, will not keep what He has purposed from coming to pass. We have God's promise that will not fail, *"all Israel will be saved* (Romans 11:26)."* The church has not replaced Israel! The true church or assembly is Israel! It may include physical descendants of Abraham, Isaac and Jacob, as well as a mixed multitude (Gentiles) **who all believe that God has provided the lamb, Yeshua/Jesus, and who will walk as He walked.**[270]

Paul tells us in 2 Thessalonians that truth is gravely important and that prior to Messiah's return, with power, signs and wonders, the lawless one will deceive many who are to perish because they ***"refused to love the truth and so be saved."***[271] The events of secular history also indicate that truth absolutely matters. Whether it be a nation, a church, or an individual, the consequence of basing one's actions on untruth is, in the end, catastrophic and leads to destruction. We've all heard the saying, "ignorance is bliss." That is not so! Not so in the past and not so now. Ignorance is a tool of Satan—it's of darkness—not of light. The world has a history of

---

[269] Ezekiel 37:15-17;

[270] 1 John 2:6 and Revelations 14:12

[271] 2 Thessalonians 2:9-10

destruction to verify the consequences of centuries of lies, deceit, hatred, prejudice, and unforgiveness. In the end, it always comes down to

"TRUTH— OR —CONSEQUENCES."

When Yeshua was being examined by the Roman governor, Pontius Pilate, he was asked the question, "What is truth?"[272] This may be the most important question in all of history! The answer to this question could bring life to a world, which is on the verge of chaos. It is imperative that believers come to an understanding of the answer. Yeshua/Jesus said, *"I am the truth!"*[273] He is the Word made flesh.[274] *"In the beginning was the Word…"*[275]

The longest chapter of the bible is Psalm 119, which has 176 verses extolling the virtues of keeping God's Law. This psalm proclaims that God's Law is true,[276] established forever,[277] and the sum of His Word is Truth.[278] The prophet Isaiah tells us that it shall come to pass in the latter days[279] that many people shall say, *"Come and let us go up to the mountain of the LORD, to the house of the God of Jacob; that He may teach us His ways and that we may walk in His path. **For out of Zion shall go forth the law, and the word of the LORD from Jerusalem** (Isaiah 2:3)."* The Truth—God's Word, God's Law—will go forth from Jerusalem and the consequence of acknowledging and accepting it will bring about the real meaning of *"…on earth peace, good will toward men."*[280] **Glory be to God!** *"And nation shall not lift up sword against nation and neither shall they learn war anymore (Isaiah 2:4)."* **Thy Kingdom come!**

---

[272] John 18:38
[273] John 14:6
[274] John 1:14
[275] John 1:1
[276] Psalm 119:142
[277] Psalm 119:152
[278] Psalm 119:160
[279] Isaiah 2:2
[280] Luke 2:14 KJV

Let's remember that the consequence for obedience is God's blessings... blessings of love, joy, contentment, abundance, good health, freedom, peace and security, all coming as a result of being in Covenant with the Creator. Obedience brings life... therefore, choose life![281]

When I chose the title, *"Truth or Consequences,"* for this book, I had absolutely no recollection for the name of "Beulah, the Buzzer." I remembered the *Truth or Consequences* TV program but couldn't remember that much about it. So, with a search on the internet, we found that the buzzer on the TV show was named "Beulah." Many Christians have heard of the song, *"Sweet Beulah Land,"*[282] but they may not be aware that the name *Beulah* comes from scripture. The word, **Beulah**, referring to the land of Israel, is mentioned only once in the Bible and is found in Isaiah when the Spirit of the Sovereign LORD came upon him and he spoke these words:

> *"For Zion's sake I will not keep silent, for Jerusalem's sake I will not remain quiet, till her righteousness shines out like the dawn, her salvation like a blazing torch. The nations will see your righteousness, and all kings your glory; you will be called by a new name that the mouth of the LORD will bestow. You will be a crown of splendor in the LORD'S hand, a royal diadem in the hand of your God. No longer will they call you Deserted, or name your land Desolate. But you will be called Hephzibah [meaning 'my delight is in her'], and your land Beulah; for the LORD will take delight in you, and your land will be married. As a young man marries a maiden so will your sons marry you; as a bridegroom rejoices over his*

---

[281] Deuteronomy 30:19
[282] Composed by Squire Parsons, Published by Benton Publishing

bride, so will your God rejoice over you (Isaiah 62:1-5 NIV). "

The glorious and triumphant victory in the "Battle for Beulah Land" is, as recorded by the prophets, in the hands of the God of Abraham, Isaac, and Jacob. For Zion's sake! For Jerusalem's sake! Israel is going to shine and be a crown of splendor in the hand of El Shaddai, the Lord God Almighty.

It seems as though God's hand is evident at times when we may least expect it. I have read this scripture before, but I was not aware of the significance or connection to "Beulah" and this book's title, *"Truth or Consequences."* With God there is no such thing as a coincidence... He is, however, full of surprises! This book's title, *"Truth or Consequences"* and "Beulah" scripturally fit the prophetic message connected to God's plan for Israel.

In Chapter One, I described the *Truth or Consequences* TV Show and Beulah, the buzzer, sounding the alarm when a contestant's time expired to answer a question. Perhaps the question today is, "Will we recognize the truth with regard to God's plan for Israel and His Kingdom with Israel's Messiah, Yeshua (Jesus), reigning as King?" Are we nearing the time in history when, instead of the sound of a buzzer, we hear the sound of a trumpet and Yeshua coming to gather His elect?

Let's note that God's plan is not a "temporary plan." Isaiah 60:21 tells us, *"Your people shall all be righteous; **they shall possess the land forever**, the shoot of my planting, **the work of my hands that I might be glorified."*** Also, let's look at Amos 9:15 where he says, *"I will plant them on their land, and **they shall never again be plucked up** out of the land which I have given them, says the Lord your God."*

I believe that by now we should realize that if God has purposed something, it's going to happen. Ignoring God's word won't make it go away!! Twisting it won't change what He said!! By looking at the Church in a rear view mirror, we have seen some of the tragic consequences of twisting and ignoring God's word. God has repeatedly warned His people through His prophets. My prayer is that the "church" would repent and be transformed from within. Judgment begins in the house of God. *"For the time has come for judgment to begin at the house of God; and if it begins with us first, what will be the end of those who do not obey the gospel of God* (1 Peter 4:17 NKJV)?*"*

Perhaps we should all park those vehicles which depart from the truth and do not rely on the word of God for fuel; then, get out and take a walk "down the Emmaus Road" with our hearts burning and minds open to His Word, His Purpose and His Truth.

Luke 24:13, 25-27 and 31-32
*"That very day two of them were going to a village named **Emmaus, about seven miles from Jerusalem. ... And He [Yeshua]** said to them, 'O foolish men and slow of heart to believe all that the prophets have spoken! Was it not necessary that the Christ should suffer these things and enter into His glory?' And beginning with Moses and all the prophets, He interpreted to them in all the scriptures the things concerning Himself. ...And their eyes were opened and they recognized Him; and He vanished out of their sight. They said to each other, 'did not our hearts burn within us while He talked to us on the road, while He opened to us the scriptures?'"*

Luke 1:31
...you shall call His name Jesus
[Yeshua, in Hebrew, means Salvation].

194

Joel 2:1; 2:32
*Blow the trumpet in Zion...for the day of the LORD
[YHVH] is coming...
... all who call upon the Name of the LORD [YHVH] shall
be delivered...*

Psalms 122:6
*Pray for the peace of Jerusalem! May they prosper who
love you!*

Shalom! Shalom Jerusalem!

Isaiah 40:1-2
*Comfort, comfort my people, says your God. Speak
tenderly to Jerusalem and cry to her that her time of warfare is
ended, that her iniquity is pardoned and that she has received
from the Lord double for all her sins.*

THE BEGINNING AND THE END

את

(The Aleph and the Tav)

**"I Am the Alpha and the Omega [Aleph and the Tav]," says
the LORD GOD,
who is and who was and who is to come, the Almighty
(Revelation 1:8)."**

THE OLD CORN HOUSE RESTORED![283]

Restoration is a good thing!

---

[283] Photo copyright 2015, Menorah Music Ministry, *The Old Corn House Restored!*

"Seek the LORD while He may be found,

Call upon Him while He is near.

Let the wicked forsake his way,

And the unrighteous man his thoughts;

Let him return to the LORD,

And He will have mercy on him;

And to our God, For He will abundantly pardon.

For My thoughts are not your thoughts,

Nor are your ways My ways," says the LORD.

"For as the heavens are higher than the earth,

So are My ways higher than your ways,

And My thoughts than your thoughts.

For as the rain comes down, and the snow from heaven,

And do not return there, But water the earth,

And make it bring forth and bud,

That it may give seed to the sower

and bread to the eater,

So shall My word be that goes forth from My mouth;

It shall not return to Me void, But it shall accomplish

what I please,

And it shall prosper in the thing for which I sent it."

Isaiah 55:6-11(NKJV)

Addendum

Jewish recipients of the Nobel Peace Prize

Literature: 1910 - Paul Heyse 1927 - Henri Bergson 1958 - Boris Pasternak 1966 - Shmuel Yosef Agnon 1966 - Nelly Sachs 1976- Saul Bellow 1978 - Isaac Bashevis Singer 1981 - Elias Canetti 1987 - Joseph Brodsky 1991 - Nadine Gordimer World 2001 – Imre Kertesz 2005 - Harold Pinter

Peace: 1911- Alfred Fried 1911 - Tobias Michael Carel Asser 1968 - Rene Cassin 1973 - Henry Kissinger 1978 - Menachem Begin 1986 - Elie Wiesel 1994 - Shimon Peres 1994 - Yitzhak Rabin 1995 – Joseph Rotblat

Economics: 1970 - Paul Anthony Samuelson 1971 - Simon Kuznets 1972 - Kenneth Joseph Arrow 1975 - Leonid Kantorovich 1976 - Milton Friedman 1978 - Herbert A. Simon 1980 - Lawrence Robert Klein 1985- Franco Modigliani 1987 - Robert M. Solow 1990 - Harry Markowitz 1990 - Merton Miller 1992 - Gary Becker 1993 - Robert Fogel 1994 – John Harsanyi 1997 - Myron Scholes 2001 – Joseph Stiglitz 2001 – George A. Akerlof 2002 – Daniel Kahneman 2002 – Daniel Kahneman 2005 – Robert Aumann 2007 – Leonid Hurwicz,Eric Maskin & Roger Myerson

Physics: 1905 - Adolph Von Baeyer 1906 - Henri Moissan 1907 - Albert Abraham Michelson 1908 - Gabriel Lippmann 1910 - Otto Wallach 1915 - Richard Willstaetter 1918 - Fritz Haber 1921 - Albert Einstein 1922 - Niels Bohr 1925 - James Franck 1925 - Gustav Hertz 1943 - Gustav Stern 1943 - George Charles de Hevesy 1944 - Isidor Issac Rabi 1952 - Felix Bloch 1954 - Max Born 1958 - Igor Tamm 1959 - Emilio Segre 1960 - Donald A. Glaser 1961 - Robert Hofstadter 1961 - Melvin Calvin 1962 - Lev Davidovich Landau 1962 - Max Ferdinand Perutz 1965 - Richard Phillips Feynman 1965 - Julian Schwinger 1969 - Murray Gell-Mann 1971 - Dennis Gabor 1972 - William Howard Stein 1973 - Brian David Josephson 1975 - Benjamin Mottleson 1976 - Burton Richter 1977 - Ilya Prigogine 1978 - Arno Allan Penzias 1978 - Peter L Kapitza 1979 - Stephen Weinberg 1979 - Sheldon Glashow 1979 - Herbert Charles Brown 1980 - Paul Berg 1980 - Walter Gilbert 1981 - Roald Hoffmann 1982 - Aaron Klug 1985 - Albert A. Hauptman 1985 - Jerome Karle 1986 - Dudley R. Herschbach 1988 - Robert Huber 1988 - Leon Lederman 1988 - Melvin Schwartz 1988 - Jack Steinberger 1989 - Sidney Altman 1990 - Jerome Friedman 1992 - Rudolph Marcus 1995 - Martin Perl 2000 - Alan J. Heeger

Chemistry: 1905 – Adolph von Baeyer 1906 – Henri Moissan 1910 – Otto Wallach 1915 – Richard Willstatter 1918 – Fritz Haber 1943 – George de Hevesy 1961 – Melvin Calvin 1962 – Max Perutz

1972 – Christian Anfinsen 1972 – William Stein 1977 – Ilya Prigogine 1979 – Herbert Brown 1980 – Paul Berg 2004 – Avram Hershko 2004 – Irwin Rose 2006 – Roger Kornberg 1980 – Walter Gilbert

1981 – Roadl Hoffmann 1982 – Aaron Klug 1985 – Herbert Hauptman 1985 – Jerome Karle 1986 – John Polanyi 1989 – Sidney Altman 1992 – Rudolph Marcus 1994 - George Olah 1996 – Harold Kroto 1998 – Walter Kohn 2000 – Alan Heeger 2004 – Aaron Ciechanover

Medicine: 1908 - Elie Metchnikoff 1908 - Paul Erlich 1914 - Robert Barany 1922 - Otto Meyerhof 1930 - Karl Landsteiner 1931 - Otto Warburg 1936 - Otto Loewi 1944 - Joseph Erlanger 1944 - Herbert Spencer Gasser 1945 - Ernst Boris Chain 1946 - Hermann Joseph Muller 1950 - Tadeus Reichstein 1952 - Selman Abraham Waksman 1953 - Hans Krebs 1953 - Fritz Albert Lipmann 1958 - Joshua Lederberg 1959 - Arthur Kornberg 1964 - Konrad Bloch 1965 - Francois Jacob 1965 - Andre Lwoff 1967 - George Wald 1968 - Marshall W. Nirenberg 1969 - Salvador Luria 1970 - Julius Axelrod 1970 - Sir Bernard Katz 1972 - Gerald Maurice Edelman 1975 - Howard Martin Temin 1976 - Baruch S. Blumberg 1977 - Roselyn Sussman Yalow 1978 - Daniel Nathans 1980 - Baruj Benacerraf 1984 - Cesar Milstein 1985 - Michael Stuart Brown 1985 - Joseph L. Goldstein 1986 - Stanley Cohen & Rita Levi-Montalcini 1988 - Gertrude Elion 1989 - Harold Varmus 1991 - Erwin Neher 1991 - Bert Sakmann 1993 - Richard J. Roberts 1993 - Phillip Sharp 1994 - Alfred Gilman 1995 - Edward B. Lewis 1997- Stanley B. Prusiner 1998 – Robert Furchgott 2000 – Paul Greengard & Eric Kandel 2002 – H. Robert Horvitz & Sydney Brenner

Notes

www.ingramcontent.com/pod-product-compliance
Lightning Source LLC
Chambersburg PA
CBHW061431040426
42450CB00007B/1006